# INCREDIBLE STUNTS

Photographs by Jeffery R. Werner

Published By

INCREDIBLE FEATURES, INC.

Printed in Korea

This book is dedicated to:

DAR ROBINSON
— The World's Greatest Stuntman —

and to

EVEL KNIEVEL
— The World's Greatest Daredevil —

Together, they inspired the work of the generations of stuntmen and daredevils who have followed.

---

AND TO MY FATHER

Harvey L. Werner, who made it all possible.

# Risky Business

GRANGER, INDIANA

Ken and John Richmond started out as a couple of normal working-class brothers from a small Indiana town. But their wild imaginations led them to invent stunts as audacious as any, most starting with John firing his 20-gauge shotgun at Ken. There are other photos in this book of John blowing a watermelon off Ken's head. But in their most dangerous stunt, John fires directly into a three-inch-thick block of concrete that Ken holds in front of his face. The shot smashes into the block at 620 mph, sending a shock wave into Ken and an explosion of concrete into the air. Shotguns are not known for accuracy in the first place, and even if they were, a minor mistake or a structural weakness in the concrete block could easily result in Ken's death. Ken and John thought it would be a piece of cake to sell this stunt to some reality show, but it was too extreme – even for American television.

# Low Rider

LOS ANGELES, CALIFORNIA

rks spray from Jim "Bullet" Bailey as he's dragged along a California runway at a skin-edding 85 mph, protected only by a fireproof suit and metal pads. Bailey invented the t in which he'd cling to a car's towbar for a quarter mile or so before letting go, ding up a shower of sparks as titanium plates scrape along the pavement. The ntegrating metal made for some great fireworks but the heat they generated was ing. This will be one of the last successful stunts that the Australian stuntman ever to celebrate. Sadly, not long after these photos were taken, Bailey decided to make azy stunt even crazier by using an airplane instead of a car to drag him down the way. Strapping himself to the undercarriage of a single-engine airplane and wearing same chest plates and protective gear, Bailey's plan was for the plane to come down land with him on it. In his first attempt at a small airstrip in Hawaii, the stunt went ust as planned. Tragically, Bailey wanted one more take for the cameras in his hopes ell the footage to the popular TV show *That's Incredible!* That proved disastrous when hook attached to the harness around Bailey's waist gave out only moments after the

# The Bus Stops Here

LAS VEGAS, NEVADA

Taking a school bus where none have gone before, Steve Hudis jumps the 28,000-pound behemoth through a giant fireball and over 15 motorcycles before crashing to earth, for the TV show *I Dare You*. After Evel Knievel pioneered and popularized the stunt of jumping buses on a motorcycle, many daredevils have followed suit. Knievel's personal best was 14 Greyhound buses parked side by side. Hudis's bus flight over 15 motorcycles was a demonstration of the reverse, if not perverse, one-upmanship that had to make even Knievel smile. The bus flew 109 feet, unexpectedly breaking a world record.

*From the files of Incredible Features, Inc.*

*www. incrediblefeatures.com*

*Incredible Stunts* by Jeffery R. Werner.

www.incrediblestunts.com

For entertainment purposes only. The events depicted in this book were performed by professionals and should not be attempted at home, or anywhere else.



Edited by Bill Graham
Produced by Stacey Linh
Designed by Jim Johnston / www.imageblast.com

Dedication page: Stunt pilot Jim Franklin with actress Judy Norton Taylor take flight over California.

First edition. Printed in Korea.

---

Werner, Jeffery R.
Incredible Stunts : The Chaos, Crashes and Courage of the World's Wildest Stuntmen & Daredevils / by Jeffery R. Werner.

ISBN 978-0-9796349-6-3

# CONTENTS

## From the Photographer...

It's always been my belief that photographers occupy an important place in culture, serving as the custodians of history; whether it be a snapshot of the minutiae of everyday life taken for personal pleasure, or a carefully planned and executed shoot, photos capture and document a single moment in time that can never truly be duplicated. Some would argue stunt photography is a frivolous occupation; I feel nothing could be further from the truth. Through the pages of this book, I have witnessed a different kind of history – I was there when Eddie Kidd jumped his motorcycle over the Great Wall of China, when Robbie Knievel passed breathlessly through the Fountains at Caesars Palace, and when pioneering movie stuntman Dar Robinson made the first high fall from a 20-story building in Miami without an airbag or parachute. These moments, no matter how fleeting, have exhilarated me and kept me searching the world for my next great subject. They have also seized the imagination and hopes of millions. To audiences and to me, these are more than stunts; they represent the pursuit of a dream and the glorious or disastrous outcomes that come from such daring pursuits. These photos are a roadmap of hope.

*Enjoy the book!*

## Acknowledgements...

A stunt may take only seconds to shoot, and hours to set up, but the contents of this book took nearly three decades to complete. There are a number of people who deserve a round of thanks for making this project, as well as my career as a stunt photographer, possible.

First and foremost, I am grateful for the many long hours of labor put in by my editor, Bill Graham. As a former photo editor and corporate director of photography for a number of publications at American Media, Bill not only assigned me many of the stunts that appear in this book, but as a great visual thinker also contributed ideas for coverage that made the shoots successful. He therefore was the obvious choice for editor of this collection. No one knows my work better, nor has a keener sense of what makes a good picture. Now living in Los Angeles, Bill is currently Director of Operations at X17 online, a large news and video agency.

Both Bill and I could not have completed this project without the guidance of Stacey Linh, who went above and beyond the call of duty in her role as producer. Stacey's professionalism in handling the marketing, advertising, editing and technical aspects shined through some of our darker moments. We also discovered that she has a great right hook that she has no problem using when we dabbled a little too long over the editing table. And she can cook.

Many thanks to Jim Johnston of Imageblast for designing a book that allows the photos to really shine. And kudos to Emma Bogren who also helped in the book's production.

Terry Caccia of Incredible Features, who assisted me on many of these shoots and physically pulled and scanned all of the pictures for the book, deserves a round of applause.

In addition, much gratitude to the wordsmiths who shaped the prose in this book, including Andy Meisler, Craig Buck, and Diedre Johnson.

I would never have gotten the opportunity to shoot some of the great stunts in this book without the help of Bruce Nash of Nash Entertainment, Gary Benz of GRB Entertainment, Alan Landsburg Productions and the production team of *Ripley's Believe It or Not.*

The following people who facilitated my career and this book including, from the world of photography: Vince Streano, Brian R. Wolff, and researcher Beth Shatsky Blount; and from the stunt world: Dar Robinson, Ky Michaelson, Kitty O'Neil, Spanky Spangler, Brian Carson, Reckless Rex, Johnnie Airtime, and of course, the great Evel Knievel, along with all the other greats found among these pages.

I'm also grateful to our panel of experts for allowing us a glimpse inside the stunt and daredevil world through the interviews found at the end of this book.

Finally, a big thank you to all the professional stunt people and daredevils who risk their lives on a daily basis to entertain us in movies, stadiums and stunt shows. Without them, there would be no James Bond, no Indiana Jones, and of course…no book.

# KING OF THE DAREDEVILS

— A Tribute to Evel Knievel —

October 17, 1938 – November 30, 2007

Photo: Heinz Kluetmeier / Sports Illustrated

"A MAN CAN FALL MANY TIMES IN LIFE, BUT HE'S NEVER A FAILURE UNTIL HE REFUSES TO GET UP."

— Evel Knievel

**ROBERT CRAIG "EVEL" KNIEVEL** was an American hero.

A pop cultural icon. A worldwide celebrity who's unique mix of courage and showmanship will undoubtedly never be matched. The trouble is that such descriptions have been repeated so often that they've become meaningless, empty hype. Sometimes, even for their truest admirers, legends, even dead ones, have to be jolted back to life.

My big jolt came a few years ago – the first week of August, 2003, to be exact.

I'd traveled to Butte, Montana – the old played-out copper mining town where Evel Knievel had been born and raised – for the second annual Evel Knievel Daze, a three-day celebration of the man himself for the people who loved him the most. The event had been barely advertised and gotten little coverage in the mainstream media. Long 'retired', Evel hadn't personally performed a stunt in more than two decades. In fact, he had ended his career at about the same time I'd begun mine.

I expected a few die-hard geezers huddled around an eclipsed star. So it was a bit of a shock when I hit town to find the place packed – 'exploding' might be a better way to put it – with nearly 80,000 spectators of every age, sex, and origin. To put things in perspective, 80,000 is almost three times Butte's permanent population. Every store and streetlamp was decorated with posters, flags, and bunting. All the hotels, bars, and restaurants were jam-packed with visitors. A large portion of the local population took the day off to join the festivities.

The first day of the event was filled with a retinue of stunt performers, like my old friends Reckless Rex, performing despite a broken foot; Spanky Spangler doing one of his signature car stunts; and a great show by the SCS Racing team; events that I, a photographer whose specialties include capturing the feats of stuntmen and daredevils, had mainly traveled there to cover.

And then, on a sunny Friday morning, with the insane roar of several hundred motorcycles lined up in two columns behind him, Evel Knievel himself – with his young blond wife, Krystal Kennedy Knievel, on the seat behind him – sat astride his immaculate custom Harley, an expression of serene magnanimity on his face. He nodded in appreciation to his thousands of fans, and they went crazy. Really crazy.

Knievel slipped his big bike into gear and pulled slowly forward to kick off the annual parade around the 'Evel Knievel Loop', an officially designated one-mile circuit around Butte that passes by important landmarks in Knievel's life.

The sidewalks were lined with thrilled spectators, four or five deep, shouting "Evel! Evel! Evel!" jumping up in the air to catch a glimpse of him. Some people – it was obvious – had come a long way for their first and only look at the King of the Daredevils. Others, just as plainly, had lived in Butte all their lives and had known Knievel since he'd been a hubcap-stealing juvenile delinquent. It made no difference; they cheered just as loudly – maybe louder. The crowds were equally divided between women and men. I recalled something Knievel once famously said: "Women want me and men want to be me."

There were hundreds of pretty young women, mostly dressed in low-cut tank tops and short skirts, many of whom hadn't even been born before Knievel stopped performing; yet here they were screaming his name and trying to get close.

Even with a camera stuck to my face, the excitement and pure magnetism of the man hit me like a bolt of lightening. I snapped as many photos of this organized chaos as I could, racing ahead to a convenient overpass to get a good overhead of the spectacular parade and its colorful leader in his rose-colored sunglasses aboard his tricked-out bike.

I shot the parade to its thunderous conclusion, then moved on to the next, even more outrageous event: an Evel Knievel look-a-like contest! It consisted of toddlers and young boys in full Evel Knievel regalia: miniature homemade red, white, and blue jumpsuits, full-face helmets, gold-tipped canes, lucky rabbits' feet – the whole deal. Their young mothers shepherded them around like groomers at a dog show.

A prepubescent redheaded lad, who lacked only a Harley to perfect his outfit, was declared the winner. By this time, the real Knievel had dismounted and waded into the crowd to sign autographs and spread handshakes, backslaps, and hugs. Jazzed by the adrenaline in the air, I got as close as I could to The Man, kneeled down, raised my camera, and shouted his name. Much to my astonishment and gratitude, Evel turned to pose for me – just for me! – for a couple of exclusive photographs. Despite years of being up-close and personal with many Hollywood celebrities, movie stars, and stuntmen, I was just as awed in the presence of Evel Knievel as everyone else in the crowd that day.

Photo: Getty Images

Photo: Getty Images

These were not my first photographs of him. I was there in 1989 when his son Robbie successfully jumped the Fountains at Caesar's Palace, after which I snapped them together in a gleeful hug. But that was a candid shot. On this day, the great Evel Knievel deigned to give up a few seconds of his life to be frozen in time by my shutter.

Photo: StillPhoto/Sunshine/Retna

On the flight home, I thought hard about how a single bike-riding senior citizen had stirred up such frenzy. On one level, I realized that with his history of record-breaking ramp-to-ramp motorcycle jumps, Evel had been the undisputed father of the entire stunt/daredevil industry. There would have been no real money for performing stunts, and none of the dozens of big stadium and halftime shows held every year, had it not been for Evel's success. It's not too much of a stretch to say that there might not be an *X-Games* or stadium motocross circuit either, not to mention a host of stunt-themed reality television shows that have come or gone over the years, many of which I worked for as their on-set photographer.

Unlike most of the young crowd in Butte that day, I was around in 1966 when Evel first jumped into the national limelight. I was barely a teenager, and a geeky one at that, but I remember it. Back then, the country was raw-edged and 'risk-averse' (to use a horrible modern-day buzzword). People didn't make waves. Society was going through changes, but so slowly that it's hard, looking back, to pinpoint when they happened. But there was nothing subtle about Evel Knievel. He burst into the public consciousness like a rocket going off.

Back then, there were no such things as side-curtain airbags, joint replacements, sports-medicine clinics, crash helmets, or even knee and elbow pads, except in football uniforms. Kids played tag and dodge ball in the schoolyard, shot cap guns with real gunpowder, scaled trees without climbing ropes, swung on jungle gyms over asphalt, skated without pads or ankle support, rode bikes without helmets, rode in cars without seatbelts, and had sparklers on their birthday cakes. Their parents shot off fireworks in their backyards on the Fourth of July. They smoked like chimneys, drank like fish, and ate with abandon until their arteries exploded. Boxers fought 15 rounds. Astronauts were hard-partying ex-fighter jocks, not electrical engineers with PhDs. It was an era of guilt-free pleasure.

A daredevil needed extremely big cojones to stand out in the crowd those days and Evel had them. He also had good looks; the magnetic personality of a born showman; and a dead-perfect nickname that not even an army of $200-an-hour ad guys could have come up with. As legend has it, his moniker was actually given to him by a jailhouse guard, and it stuck.

Then, there was the fabled Knievel back story: abandoned by his parents as a toddler and raised by his grandparents to become the high-school dropout biker that every local mother warned her daughter about; then 'growing up' to become a failed copper miner, insurance salesman, burglar, and Honda dealer; finally finding his true calling. He mustered his athletic skills and his tremendous courage to launch himself, and his 1000-pound Triumph 750 motorcycle, into the unknown.

The idea had been kindled by a childhood memory of the Joie Chitwood Thrill Show. He recalled how awestruck he had been with the death-defying automobile stunts of Chitwood's 'Hell Drivers'. That memory from a happier

Photo: Bettman Corbis

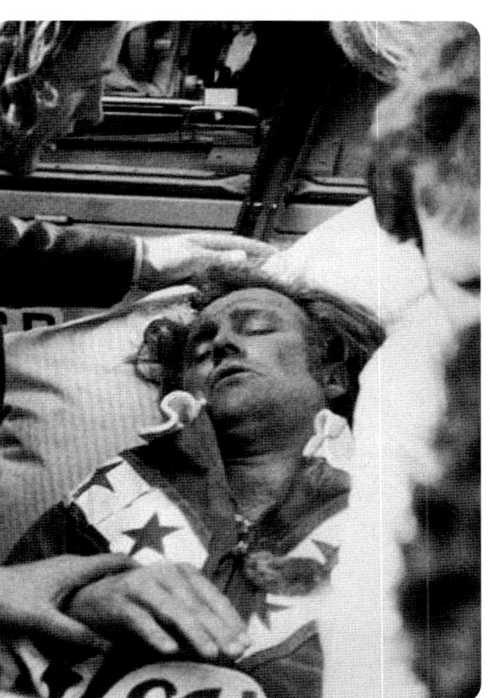

Photo: Getty Images

**ABOVE:** Evel Knievel starred as himself in 1977's *Viva Knievel!,* here pictured with his co-star Lauren Hutton.

**SEQUENCE:** Knievel's May 1975 disastrous attempt to jump 120 feet over 13 buses at Wembley in London drew over 90,000 spectators into the stadium, "more people than they ever drew there for a soccer game between any two countries," he later commented. Despite problems with his gearing, the daredevil went ahead with the jump, barely clearing the 13 buses only to crash upon landing, ending up with a concussion and fractured pelvis. "My grandma always taught me to catch the last bus," he wisecracked from his stretcher.

Photo: Bettman Corbis

past is often credited as the inspiration for Evel's first major stunt: jumping his bike over two mountain lions and 100 rattlesnakes to publicize his motorcycle shop. The stunt worked, but the shop went out of business anyway. Nevertheless the buzz he got from the audience's reaction opened his eyes to a whole new career. Evel Knievel: Daredevil.

Evel's jumps involved no special effects or illusions. No steroids or mind-altering drugs were involved. In fact, he was a prominent early advocate of 'Just Say No To Drugs' and spoke against drug abuse at many of his performances. Knievel actually bet his life every time he roared up his takeoff ramp. And he had the medical records to prove it.

Starting at small venues in Central California, he worked his way toward stadium shows up and down the West Coast. He collected hordes of new fans by jumping over cars, buses, or Pepsi-cola trucks. But when he came up short, as he did more often then not, he also left a trail of splintered limbs, ribs, clavicles, shredded cartilage, torn tendons, and mashed internal organs.

Knievel remained relatively non-bionic until December 31, 1967, when his epochal near-miss of a 141-foot jump over the fountains in the courtyard of Caesar's Palace in Las Vegas resulted in too many broken bones to count, a 29-day coma, and the desire of an enthralled TV audience to see him get screwed, welded, and spliced back together, making him just well enough to get back on his bike and try to break his own records. He continued to do just that through the early 1980s – even after the ignominious failure of his rocket-powered X-2 Skycycle to clear Idaho's Snake River Canyon in 1974. Yet despite that failure, the fact that he even attempted that seemingly impossible stunt burnished Evel's legend even further.

No one knows how many broken bones Evel suffered during his career. The number is shrouded in mystery, much like the legend himself. The general consensus is that he broke somewhere between 35 and 40 bones and sustained up to 430 fractures, winning him a spot in the Guinness Book of World Records. At the end of his career, Evel referred to his body as "nothing but scar tissue and surgical steel." The man made at least 300 jumps in his career – many

**ABOVE:** The stunt that made Evel Knievel a household name occurred on December 31, 1967 in Las Vegas, Nevada. The daredevil's attempt to jump over the Fountains at Caesars Palace resulted in his most famous crash and landed him in a coma for 29 days.

**BELOW:** Knievel sits in the cockpit of the X-2 Skycycle right before take-off over the Snake River Canyon in Idaho on September 8, 1974.

Photo: Associated Press

# MOTORCYCLE MAYHEM

MOJAVE DESERT, CALIFORNIA

Veteran aerial stuntman Jimmy Lynn Davis bails out of the back of a cargo plane at 5,000 feet with two parachutes, one for him, and one for the motorcycle that he flies down to the earth for a successful two-wheeled landing.

Photo: Alan Landsburg Productions / Incredible Features

# Human Wrecking Ball

SIOUX FALLS, SOUTH DAKOTA

Imagine roaring off a motorcycle ramp at 120 mph, soaring into the sky high enough to fly over more than 50 cars, and suddenly knowing you're not going to make it. In this incredible sequence, stunt cyclist John Holland faces this frightening realization in a world record attempt gone horribly wrong. With a top speed of 126 mph, Holland hopes his powerful 560-pound Yamaha XS1100 will propel him 265 feet over the cars and onto his landing ramp, where two parachutes will open to slow him down. But nothing in this stunt goes according to plan. Seconds into the jump, Holland realizes that he has no chance of reaching the speed that he needs to make the ramp. His only chance at survival is to risk opening the chutes in mid-air and praying for the best. The chutes rip him off the bike, sending him crashing into the cars with such violence that his body buckles one of the roofs and knocks several cars off their wheels. His momentum bounces him repeatedly through showers of exploding glass as the audience screams in horror. Unconscious by now, Holland crashes into his ramp and ricochets over it, falling hard on the unforgiving tarmac below. Rescue teams rush to the stuntman's limp body and are amazed to find him still breathing, though just barely. Holland spends nearly a year in the hospital, recovering from massive injuries, ending his stunt career for good.

**FAR LEFT:** Holland's second, larger parachute jerks him off his bike with violent force, sending him smashing into the cars he had planned to jump.

**LEFT:** In the next shot, Holland's body, traveling at close to 100 mph, bounces like a basketball off the hard steel of the cars, high into the air.

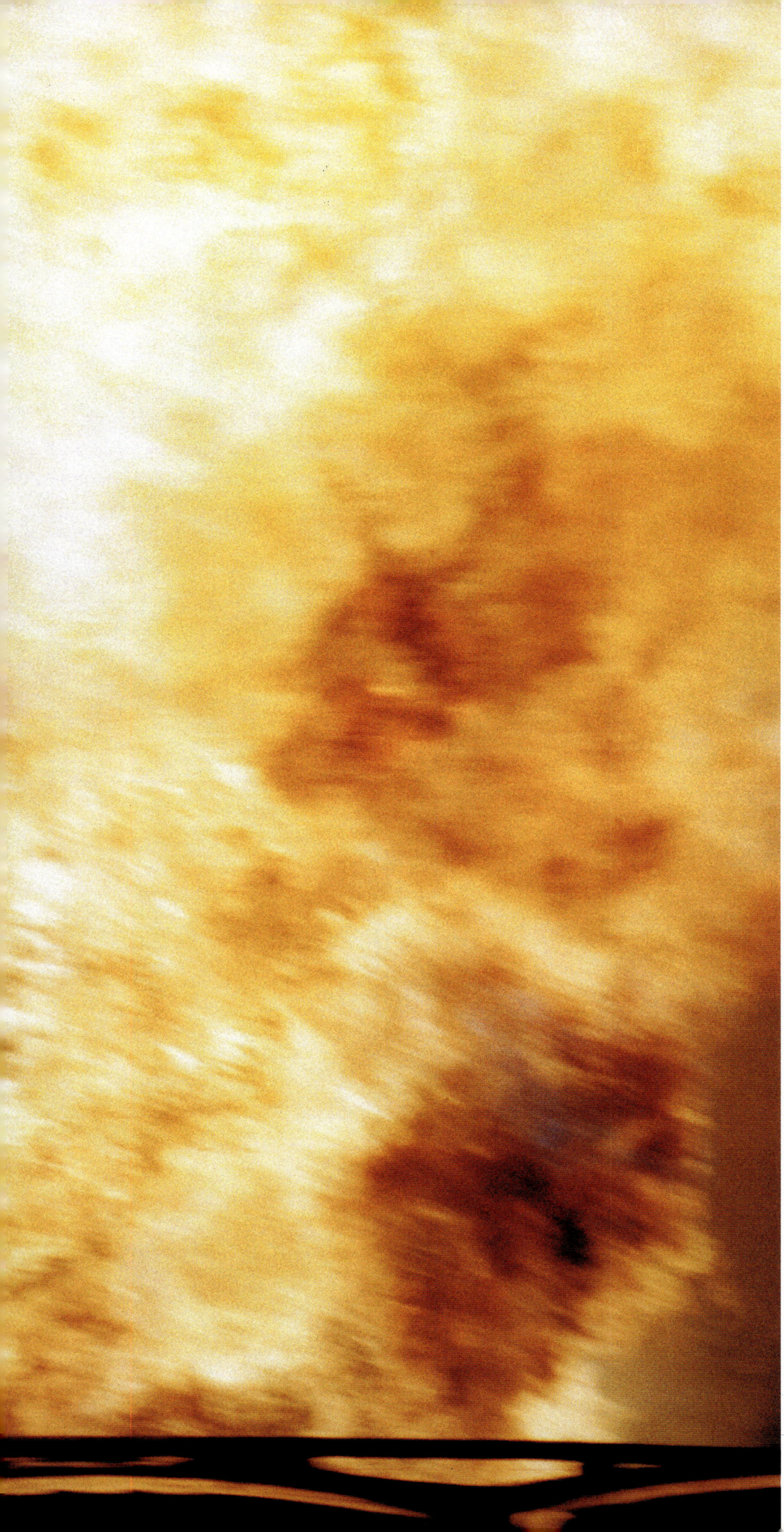

# E.T. Phone Home

LAS VEGAS, NEVADA

In a scene reminiscent of the movie E.T., firebombs provide an explosive backdrop for stuntman Bubba Blackwell, as he jumps his Harley Davidson 750 over 15 buses lined up side-by-side. With a crew from the *I Dare You* television show recording the action, Blackwell steers his bike up a 4-foot wide, 80-foot long ramp at 95 mph to fly 130 feet over the buses for a new world record. The successful stunt broke the previous record of 14 buses, held for 25 years by Blackwell's hero, Evel Knievel. Knievel had set that record in a comeback after a 13-bus crash at London's Wembley Stadium in 1975.

# Pocket Rocket

MOJAVE DESERT, CALIFORNIA

When the hit TV show *That's Incredible!* had a performer injured during a fire tunnel gag in their first season, they turned to legendary stuntman Dar Robinson to safely coordinate their action shots for the second season. This stunt, featuring Tracy Smith rocketing over a 150-foot cardboard tunnel, is Dar's first effort for the show. His fire team waited until Smith was approaching the tunnel at 80 mph before setting it ablaze. I catch the shot by triggering a remote shutter, before jumping from the top of a fire truck to clear the area. The unmanned camera with a telephoto lens catches Smith, in this classic photo, hovering between two lips of flame and smoke. The TV crew is not so lucky: Though the stunt is successful, it has to be re-staged the next day, because the fire tunnel got so hot, so fast, that the crew is forced to escape the blaze before completing their shot.

# HELL'S KITCHEN

LAS VEGAS, NEVADA

In this action sequence for TV's *I Dare You*, stuntman Nick Plantico takes a ride through hell itself, or at least through a 210-foot section of it. Wearing a fire-retardant suit and helmet, the toughest part of the stunt for Plantico turns out to be the smoke from the burning haystacks. Unable to see, he loses control near the end of the inferno and crashes just short of his goal. Nick escapes with only burns on the back of his neck, thanks to the speed and competence of his safety crew

# TRIPLE THREAT

JOSHUA TREE, CALIFORNIA

3 Ramps + 3 Stuntmen = 1 Great Jump. 'Crazy' Dave Lott and Michael Brown make a daring mid-air criss-cross on motorcycles over an airborne car driven by Shawn Wolf on a dry lakebed. Employing three separate take-off ramps, the stuntmen must calculate their speed, timing, and height down to the second in order to avoid a potentially deadly collision. The result is this perfectly timed picture and a big thumbs-up from Wolf.

# Falling Short

OXFORD, MICHIGAN

Rod Woodworth's dream of becoming a daredevil is smashed, along with many of his bones, when he attempts to jump a motorbike 180 feet over 32 cars near his family's home in Michigan. Woodworth guns his cycle and hits the takeoff ramp at 93 mph – fast but not fast enough. His back tire snags the last car, sending his bike careening into the landing ramp, hurling him off the bike and skipping like a stone across the hard-packed dirt road. An ambulance whisks him away for emergency treatment. "It was the most frightening moment of my life," says the would-be daredevil during his 12-day hospital stay.

THE ULTIMATE
CHALLENGE
L·1011

# Flying First Class

KINGMAN, ARIZONA

Motorcycle daredevils are always scratching their heads, trying to come up with new obstacles to jump. For this stunt, Doug Danger decides to take on the entire wingspan of a large-body L1011 passenger jet, an impressive 160-foot jump, for the TV show *I Dare You*. Danger, who previously broke the ramp-to-ramp world record of 42 cars, 251 feet, needs this stunt to work. It is his comeback jump, after a crash in 1992 left him in a coma with 17 major fractures including his skull, femur, tibia, and fibula – not to mention a three-year struggle to regain his memory. With a 4-foot-wide takeoff ramp, an 8-foot landing ramp, and a strong headwind, it looks likely that Danger's latest jump might end up much like his last. But instead, the appropriately named Danger makes the stunt look easy, reaching the pre-calculated speed of 73 mph to launch himself off the 120-foot long narrow ramp, straight up and over the parked jumbo. "I'm still number one!" he roars upon landing.

VALLEY
YAMAHA
BMW

## Watery Splashdown

SPOKANE, WASHINGTON

"Remember this: Reckless Rex is a true daredevil," Evel Knievel said to me in our last conversation before his death. His friend and supporter for many years, Reckless Rex Phelps, proves his hero's words in this unique take on motorcycle jumping. Phelps purposefully rides his bike up a steep ramp and into a barrier at 60 mph to propel himself into the air like a human rocket. Standing upright on the seat, he catapults 138 feet over 12 cars, splashes down in Willow Bay, and sets a new world record in the process, besting Knievel's longest jump of 129 feet... and Knievel stayed on his bike!

# BACKSPLASH

SPOKANE, WASHINGTON

Reckless Rex Phelps pioneered motorcycle backflips, preferring splashdowns in lakes or pools to splatting on hard surfaces. For this stunt, at Willow Bay Resort, Phelps speeds his Yamaha DT175MX up a steep and narrow ramp at 40 mph, propelling him high into the air. But things start to go wrong when he tries to perform a complete somersault. Phelps loses control of the bike and makes a 35-foot dive into the water. His bike comes down fast, almost hitting him, before splashing into the lake and drenching some hapless photographer (namely me). Phelps is not hurt in this mishap but suffers serious injuries performing a similar stunt for a show in Seattle, some years later, when he hits the edge of a water tank.

# Back 'Em Up

MARTINSVILLE, INDIANA

Roger Ridell, aka 'Mr. Backwards', steers his bike in a most unusual way — riding with his back facing the handlebars so that he can't see where he's going. For a show in Indiana, he successfully clears five cars. But when he tries for six, he crashes on the landing ramp. Suffering from a cracked rib, Ridell rides forward all the way to the hospital, but this time in an ambulance.

## Fearless Flyer

LANCASTER, CALIFORNIA

Master motorcycle aerialist Johnny Airtime sets a world record by jumping four Robinson R22 helicopters - with their blades spinning! One false move and he's shredded. This stunt was filmed for Fox TV's *The Ultimate Challenge*.

# 360 Degree Flip That Flopped

TUCSON, ARIZONA

Jose Yanez was the first BMX star to manage a bicycle backflip in 1984, but translating that skill to a motorcycle proves more difficult, not to mention more dangerous. Flying skyward from the curved ramp, Yanez loses control of his Suzuki RM80 in mid-air. He smashes hard onto the ramp, flat on his back, and then his bike flips over on top of him. Unbelievably, this dramatic crash leaves Yanez merely winded.

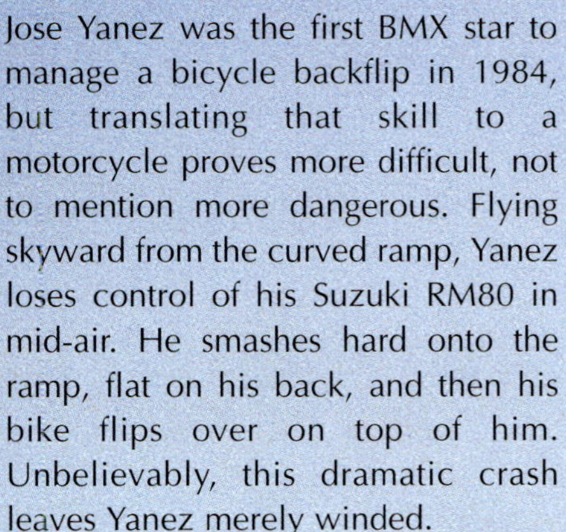

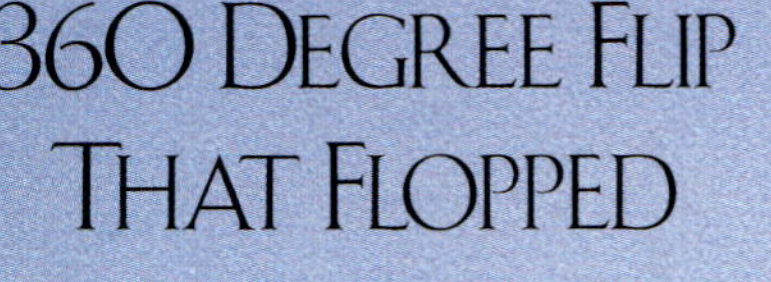

# THE GREAT WALL OF CHINA JUMP

NEAR BEIJING, CHINA

It has taken two years for famed English stuntman Eddie Kidd to receive permission from the Chinese government to risk this triumphant jump over the Great Wall of China, but the day has finally come. Before a crowd of 35,000 onlookers, Kidd's greatest challenge is a blind landing on a crude bamboo ramp that is perched precariously over the deadly river far below, which is hidden from view beyond the wall at the end of the jump. A miscalculation or a sudden gust of wind can carry Kidd off course, causing him to miss the narrow ramp and plunge 600 feet to his death. Luckily, the former James Bond stuntman hits the ramp with only inches to spare, making the 33-foot leap over one of the world's seven wonders and crashing into a safety barrier made of cardboard boxes. This stunt is a huge success and a career high for Kidd. But three years later, in 1996, the veteran of 3,000 jumps suffers serious head and pelvic injuries in a stunt crash in the UK. Kidd is disabled for more than a decade, but never daunted, he makes a comeback in 2007, opening the Beyond Boundaries Live Exhibition at Sundown Park, aboard a Conquest 1200 motorcycle.

# Dodging Death On The Rails

PARKDALE, OREGON

In this heart-stopping stunt, motorcycle aerialist Johnny Airtime doesn't just soar an incredible 180 feet over three train cars, he does it while they're moving! Racing down the track at 80 mph, he roars up a steep wooden ramp as the oncoming train, moving at 23 mph, heads right towards him! The train demolishes the ramp within a heartbeat of Airtime's takeoff. Airtime sails high over the train, aiming for a landing ramp alongside the track. This amazing jump was performed for a Fox TV special, *Live! The World's Greatest Stunts*.

UNION PACIFIC

# For Better Or Worse

DENVER, COLORADO

Sparks flew when French stuntman Reno Jaton met his future wife, Cleo, at an Arkansas air show, and ever since, they've been flying for real. The couple now tours together performing a variety of dangerous acrobatic stunts, both on and off their motorcycles. Reno holds the quarter-mile world record for being dragged on pavement behind a 14,000-horsepower jet car, reaching 236 mph, subjecting his body to at least 6 Gs, and enduring the spitting flames of the jet engine that reached 700-degrees Fahrenheit. While Cleo – who learned all of her motorcycle skills from her husband – holds several records herself, including the world's fastest female pavement skier. She opens their daredevil shows by standing upright and balancing on a speeding cycle while holding an American flag in one hand.

Meguiar's
SEGURA
EBC
Reno
AIRVEST

# Two T-Bones Please

TUNICA, MISSISSIPPI (BELOW) AND CHARLOTTE, NORTH CAROLINA (RIGHT)

Dennis Pinto is the master of the T-bone stunt, where he crashes a motorcycle smack into a bus or a van to rocket himself airborne. To make the stunt even more exciting, not to mention challenging, Pinto wears a flame-retardant outfit and either lights himself on fire or flies through massive pyro explosions. In the stunt below, Pinto's fiery flight over a school bus proves a bit too ambitious. The stuntman misses his soft target of piled-up cardboard boxes and crash lands on the hard pavement instead, breaking several bones in the process. To the right, his crash into a parked van is more successful, as he hurtles through the flames and lands on his intended cardboard buffer.

# Kitecycle Truck Bounce

KINGMAN, ARIZONA

Take a motorcycle, add a hang-glider, and you've got a "kitecycle" that looks like it came straight out of Wile E. Coyote's workshop. Daredevil Bob Correll has been wowing stunt show crowds since the 70s with this famous machine, designed by partner Doug Malewicki, who also created the skycycle for Evel Knievel's unsuccessful Snake River jump. After a lengthy retirement, Correll attempts a record-breaking comeback with this 280-foot jump over four tractor-trailers. With no instruments to gauge his speed, his bike races up the takeoff ramp at only 63 mph, not the 90 mph that he needs to successfully complete the jump. Correll crashes into the cab of the fourth truck, spins out-of-control, and crashes hard onto the pavement below. Paramedics help the dazed stuntman into an ambulance, but remarkably his injuries are not serious.

I DARE YOU!
THE ULTIMATE CHALLENGE
I DARE YOU!
THE ULTIMATE CHALLENGE

# INTO THE AIR

FAYETTEVILLE, WEST VIRGINIA

In this sequence shot for FOX-TV's *World's Greatest Stunts,* aerial stunt specialist Jake Lombard attempts a catapult jump from a bridge onto a moving airplane and misses by just inches! Luckily, he deploys his parachute just in time to break his 875 foot fall. Lombard has performed several aerial stunts for James Bond movies.

# Flying Standby

MOJAVE, CALIFORNIA

What can a passenger do if the flight is booked solid? Canadian daredevil Rick Rojatt, who likes to hide behind the anonymous billing of 'The Human Fly', has one rather outlandish solution: In a red mask and white cape, Rojatt, with his legs and chest strapped to the plane by cables, stands upright on top of a DC-8 while it flies over the California desert at 250 mph. In order to withstand the 3,000 pounds of air pressure at take-off, he wears a helmet and steel-reinforced jumpsuit and breathes through oxygen tubes. Unfortunately, a helmet visor pops up during a dive, exposing his eyes to the wind, but Rojatt perseveres. "He did a lot of squinting," says the pilot, Clay Lacy, who watched The Fly on closed circuit TV from the cockpit. The Human Fly carries the distinction of being the only character found in the Marvel Comics series that is based on an actual person.

# Double Trouble

PORTLAND, OREGON

Cathi Reavis and Connie Warren are the wing-walking duo better known as the 'Daring Damsels'. Together with Warren's husband Bill who pilots the 1941 vintage biplane, the Damsels perform breath-taking stunts while zipping through the skies at 180 mph at air shows around the U.S. and Canada. Shooting from another open-cockpit plane that is flying only a few feet away in the photo to the right, my challenge is to get the shots without asphyxiating on the biplane's fuel fumes.

DAMSELS

# PASSING THE BATON

EL TORO, CALIFORNIA

At 4,000 feet above the ground, soaring within inches of each other at 120 mph, Johnny Kasian and Lori Lynn Ross trust their lives to precision pilots Eliot Cross and Jim Franklin. The pilots must fly their biplanes with faultless accuracy so that Ross, who hangs upside down from Cross's inverted plane, can successfully pass the baton to Kazian below. It would take only a tiny pilot error to result in a fatal midair collision. The planes look like mirror images in the split second that both wing-walkers have hold of the baton.

# On A Wing And A Prayer

VANCOUVER, WASHINGTON

While other air daredevils use parachutes, safety straps, steel-reinforced flight suits, and other protective equipment, Mary Ella McIlvain, a 52-year old grandmother of three walks the wing of a biplane, 1,000 feet in the air, wearing only a sundress. While she may appear to be an unlikely daredevil, this secretary got tired of being deskbound and took to the air. Below, she works her way out to midwing of a WWI Curtiss Jenny biplane, flown by 75-year old Wally Olson, having nothing more than the plane's normal wires and struts to hold onto.

## Truck Stop

LAS VEGAS, NEVADA

Any pilot can land a plane on a runway, especially if it's a 1956 Mooney M-20 like this one. But it takes extreme skill to land it in the back of a semi-truck driving 65 mph along a dusty, dry lakebed. Pilot Craig Hoskins proves that he has the right stuff for this unusual stunt. Neither Hoskins nor Bobby Orr, who's driving the truck, is injured during the filming of this segment of the *I Dare You* TV series. Though they do get a lot of stares from passing motorists.

# Home Wrecker

LANCASTER, CALIFORNIA

Instead of flying by the seat of his pants, sky jockey Jim Lasley plants his on the living room couch in this explosive stunt that literally brings down the house. For a segment televised on *That's Incredible!,* Lasley flies a small plane into a house at 60 mph tearing the aircraft's wings away and destroying the structure. Before the dust settles, rescue crews rush to Lasley's aid, but he emerges from the decimated plane unhurt.

# Airplane Transfer

MOJAVE DESERT, CALIFORNIA

At El Mirage Dry Lakebed, California-Legendary stuntman Dar Robinson performs a car-to-airplane transfer stunt for the TV series *The Fall Guy*. Withstanding 80 mph winds, Robinson stands in the back of a convertible, directs the pilot of a low-flying biplane through the dangerous maneuver of aligning the aircraft just inches from the speeding car, launches himself onto a strut, hauls himself onto the wing, and then works his way into the front cockpit for the flight home.

RESTRICTED

# HEAD RUSH

REIMS, FRANCE

Floating 1,000 feet above French farmland, aerial acrobat Veronique Gougat dangles gracefully from a hot air balloon, performing acrobatic stunts without any safety wires to break her surely-fatal fall should she lose her balance or her grip. During two early morning shoots, I go up first in another balloon to shoot Gougat as she climbs down from the basket, mounts the trapeze, and proceeds to hang upside-down by her feet above a forest. The next morning, I hang a long pole with a camera attached over the side of the balloon's basket and use a remote trigger to shoot her hanging upside down with her legs and in another shot, holding on with only one hand while looking up at the camera. Because I can't see her from my angle without climbing out of the basket myself, I have Gougat yell "shoot" whenever she is ready for her close-up.

BULLE D'OR

# Breaking The Ground Barrier

ALBUQUERQUE, NEW MEXICO

Strapped to the top wing of a 1940s biplane at 180 mph, 53-year old wing-walker Johnny Kazian is flipped upside-down by stunt pilot Jim Franklin. Franklin then flies the inverted plane so close to the ground that Kazian is actually below ground level in a drainage ditch where he snatches a red ribbon stretched across the ditch.

Sadly, Franklin died in a midair crash at an air show in Moose Jaw, Saskatchewan, on July 10, 2005.

Photos: Jeffery R. Werner with Jamie Budge for Incredible Features, Inc.

N23690

# HIGHFALLS

COEUR D' ARLENE, IDAHO

Stuntman Jeff Habberstad is lit on fire and jumps 192 feet from a building's balcony, engulfed in flames, to land on an air bag. He had suffered third degree burns only a week earlier while practicing for this stunt, shot for the TV show *Stuntmasters*.

# HIGH ROLLER

LAS VEGAS, NEVADA

Stuntman Dan Koko breaks two world records in three months from the top of Vegas World. In the first, he is set on fire and plummets 311 feet at an astounding 88 mph into an air bag. He shatters the old jump record by nearly 8 stories while setting a new fire-fall record at the same time. Three months later, in his second attempt, without fire this time, Koko builds a special platform on the roof of Vegas World to increase the height and dive into a new record at 326 feet. Koko lands on an air bag that is set to 'explode' upon impact; air is forced into the bag at up to 700 mph to keep the force of Koko's falling body from deflating the 25-foot tall bag. "I don't think of it in terms of feet," says Koko, "I look at it by time — seconds, not distance. The 326 foot fall was only one and a half seconds." For his second effort, Koko received a cool $1 million in cash, from Vegas World owner Bob Stupak.

# He Fell Through A Burning Ring Of Fire

CHARLOTTE, NORTH CAROLINA

As 60,000 people held their breath, stuntman Spanky Spangler stands 150 feet atop a crane, staring at an air bag that from his vantage point looks like a postage stamp. An assistant lights Spangler on fire and he does a swan dive from the crane, through an explosion, falling 150 feet into the air bag. The flames are so intense they nearly set the air bag on fire, but after being doused with flame retardant, Spangler emerges unhurt.

# Free Falling

LOS ANGELES, CALIFORNIA

Kitty O'Neil, the world's most famous stuntwoman, steps out onto the strut of a helicopter and takes a flying leap from an altitude of 180 feet. She makes a perfect landing on her back, in the center of an air bag. A miss, by even a foot could have been fatal. O'Neil is also the 'world's fastest woman' in a rocket car. Stockard Channing portrayed the deaf stuntwoman in the TV movie *Silent Danger: The Kitty O'Neil Story.*

# FREE FALLING PART DEUX

LOS ANGELES, CALIFORNIA

A few years after Kitty O'Neil broke the world high fall record, fellow American Indian stuntwoman Allison Logsdon makes another helicopter jump to break O'Neil's record by 11 feet. Under the tutelage of Hollywood stuntman Dar Robinson, Logsdon jumps from the chopper to an air bag 191 feet below for a 3-point landing. During a practice run, Logsdon hit the side of the airbag from a lower altitude, escaping death only by inches.

# "STICK" IT!

MIAMI, FLORIDA

Dar Robinson was an innovative stuntman who helped revolutionize Hollywood movie stunts. He and Ky 'Rocket Man' Michaelson designed and built a drum and cable system called a decelerator, to enable a stuntman to jump off of a high building and land unharmed, without the aid of the traditional air bag. Dar first used this system in the movie *Stick*, starring Burt Reynolds. In this stunt, Dar leaps from the 20th floor of a hotel and free-falls until the brake on the cable drum brings him to an abrupt but safe stop a couple of stories above the pavement below. This innovative system allows the cameras to shoot from overhead without having an airbag in the shot. After Dar's death, his protege, Kenny Bates, went on to use this system for the famous leap from the top of a Los Angeles skyscraper in the movie *Die Hard*.

# ON FIRE

MANKATO, MINNESOTA

Stuntman Gary Beal, protected by a fire-retardant suit, escapes in a blaze of glory after an explosion engulfs the car in a blanket of flames that trails him as he walks away unscathed.

## Dressed For Success

SACRAMENTO, CALIFORNIA

Two-time Stuntman of the Year and eight world record holder Ricky D cheats death, and does so in style, as he jumps through a 900-degree Fahrenheit wall of fire at 55 mph, wearing a $1,500 Pierre Cardin tuxedo! A thumbs up after landing signals yet another world record. D suffers minor burns when a flaming piece of wood catches his arm as he bursts through the inferno on his 65-horsepower jet ski. Ricky D's only complaint? "It's the quickest way I know to ruin a perfectly good tux."

Ricky 'D'
JETCO

# Trouble Down Under

BRISBANE, AUSTRALIA

World water-skiing champion Geoff Carrington's body flops around like a rag doll as he flies through flaming wreckage in this stunt gone horrifically wrong! As the ski boat slams deliberately into the pier, Carrington shoots off a ramp that is supposed to launch him over the crash. Instead, he loses control, falls short, and hits the dock at a bone-crunching 50 mph. By the time he plunges headfirst into the lake, he is unconscious. Carrington is comatose for several months after the disaster and spends more than a year recovering.

Photos: Patrick Riviere for Incredible Features, Inc.

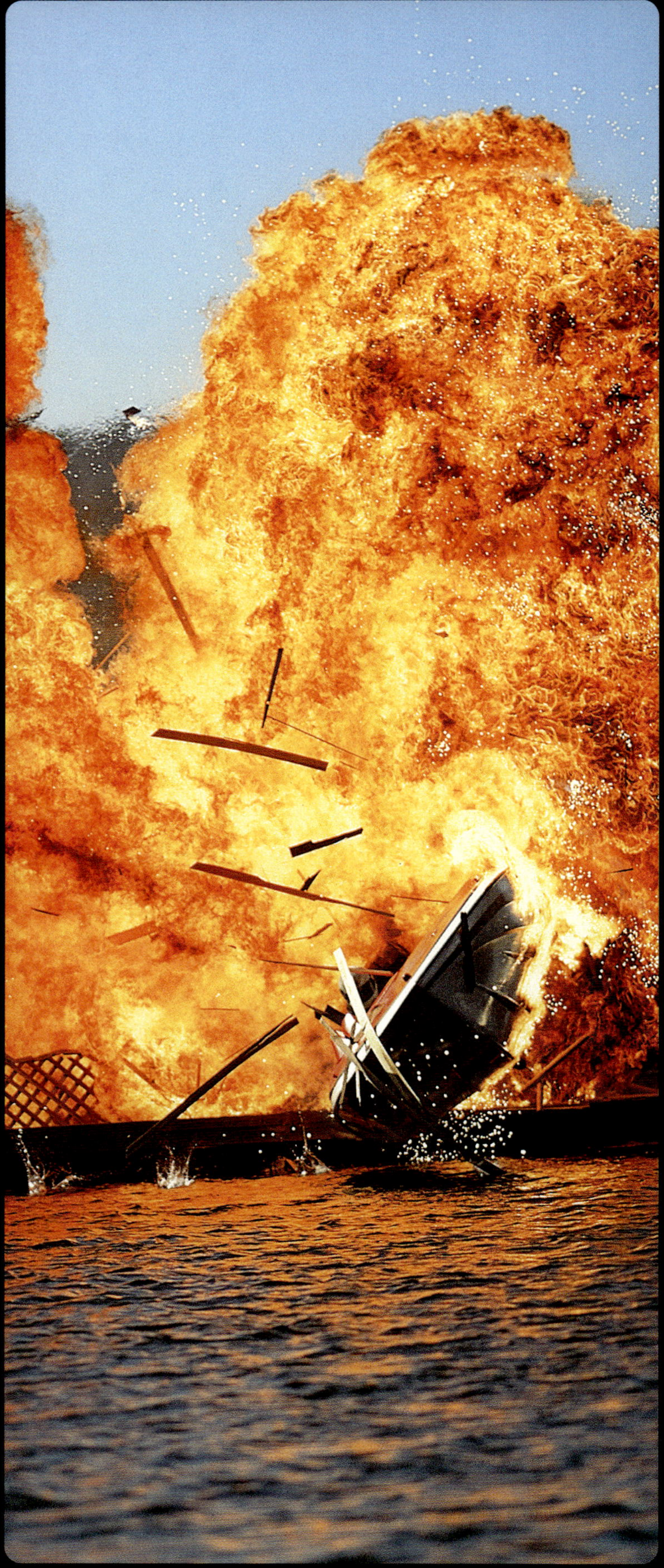

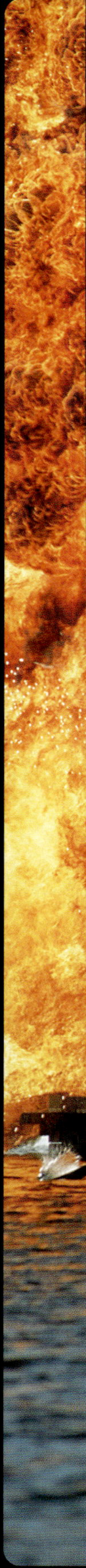

# FIERY GAZEBO

LAKE COEUR D'ALENE, IDAHO

Stuntman Mickey Giacomazzi achieves his burning ambition while filming for the TV show *Stuntmasters*. Giacomazzi speeds his custom-equipped boat at 60 mph up a ramp to fly airborne for 20 feet, before smacking into an exploding gazebo. Onlookers held their breath until Giacomazzi roared out of the flames, smiling and unscathed thanks to a specially designed roll cage, fireproof outer structure, and sealed gas tank.

## AIR RAM FLIP

PALMDALE, CALIFORNIA

Dennis 'Danger' Madalone gets all fired up during a shoot for the *Stuntmasters* TV show, where Madalone plays a terrorist being blown up by a hand grenade. To simulate this effect, he is first set on fire by the stunt crew, before running over an air ram hidden in the ground. The ram hurls the flaming stunt man 35 feet through the air, landing in a pool to douse the flames. Madalone is best known for his work on *Star Trek: Next Generation* as well as *The X-Files*.

## HARD LANDING

OWATONNA, MINNESOTA

In this stunt gone south, daredevil Jack McElrath is perched atop a flaming car that has been vertically propped up against a parked car, as fellow daredevil Gary Beall races toward him at 65 mph in yet a third car. McElrath jumps off the upright car as it goes up in flames but misses his intended target - a mud pit, and lands face down on the parked car instead. His body smashes the rear windshield as the upright car explodes in a giant fireball beside him. Miraculously, he walks away unharmed.

SWINE
AMZ 964

# Human Fireball

MOJAVE DESERT, CALIFORNIA

Steve Neale becomes a fiery flesh-and-blood torch when the shocked stuntman plunges headfirst through the heat-weakened windshield of the car roaring towards him at 50 mph. Even with Neale's careful planning, this stunt for *Stuntmaster's* TV show proves far from foolproof! If the stunt went according to plan, Neale should have been flung off the hood on impact and onto the roof to safety. Instead, he gets stuck inside the car's raging inferno, with the gel on his suit blazing like a marshmallow. Still on fire, he manages to extricate himself from the car as the safety team runs up to douse the flames.

# LIMOUSINE LEAPFROG

LAS VEGAS, NEVADA

Stuntman Nick Plantico plays a dangerous game of leapfrog, accelerating his black Pontiac Firebird at 55 mph toward a parked limousine. Cannons mounted in the front and rear of the limo are remotely fired at the last moment, shooting the heavy vehicle 20 feet into the air to allow Plantico to race through the flames beneath it. At the same time, gasoline bombs go off to flood the scene with explosions. Plantico has barely a second to complete the stunt before the three-ton limo comes crashing back to earth.

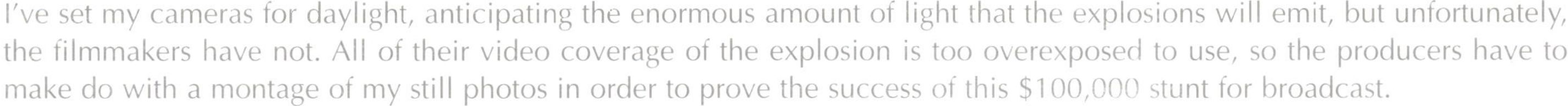

I've set my cameras for daylight, anticipating the enormous amount of light that the explosions will emit, but unfortunately, the filmmakers have not. All of their video coverage of the explosion is too overexposed to use, so the producers have to make do with a montage of my still photos in order to prove the success of this $100,000 stunt for broadcast.

# Pipe Dreams

LOS ANGELES, CALIFORNIA

Stuntmen Pat Statham and Kurt Bryant perform a death-defying double pipe ramp roll and fire stunt for the Roger Corman Film *Black Scorpion 2*. The scene calls for the two police cars to chase the Black Scorpion's car, driven by Pat Statham's wife Ellen. It loses control and runs into a garbage dumpster, then flies through the air and explodes into flames. The pipe ramps are designed to angle the cars so that they twist when they launch into the air. The two cars hit the ramps at 55 mph and corkscrew through an explosive fire. They land hard and fire crews rush in to extinguish the flames. Both drivers walk away, though Pat suffers a tiny cut on his finger and jokingly calls for the paramedics.

# Freezer Burn

WRIGHTWOOD, CALIFORNIA

Stuntman Jay Currin hot dogs his way through a 25-foot fireball of flaming gasoline in this spectacular snowboarding stunt at Mountain High Ski Resort. Currin flies through the inferno with his clothes ablaze, then sails through the air leaving a trail of smoke behind him. He lands hard, but luckily his safety crew gets there in time to extinguish the flames. Sadly, Currin is killed a year later rehearsing for a movie stunt in Malibu when he misses the air bag during a high fall off a boulder.

YOUR
SOLINGEN INDUSTRIAL CORP

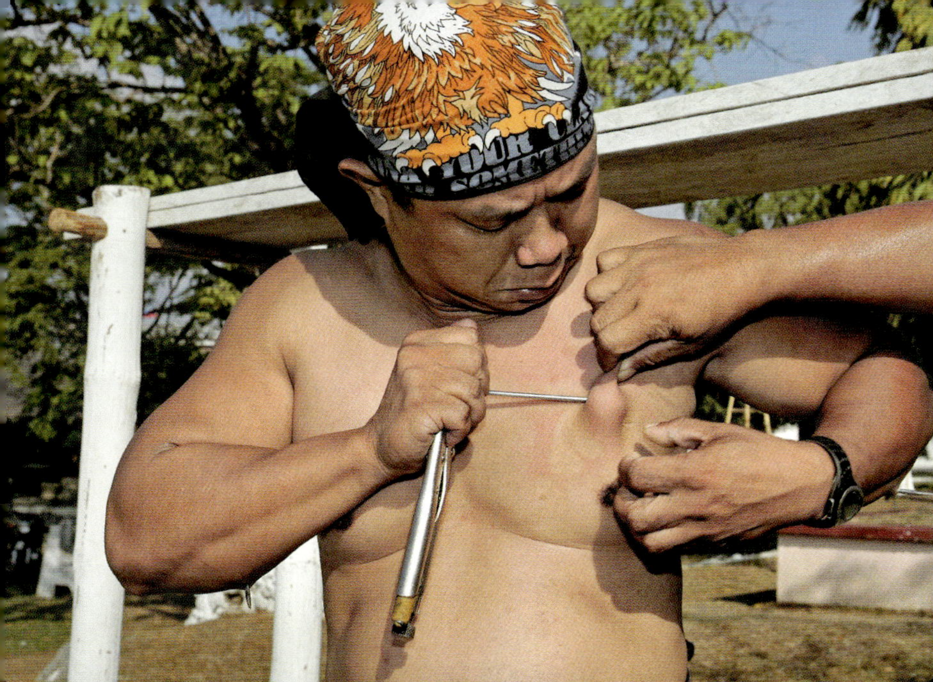

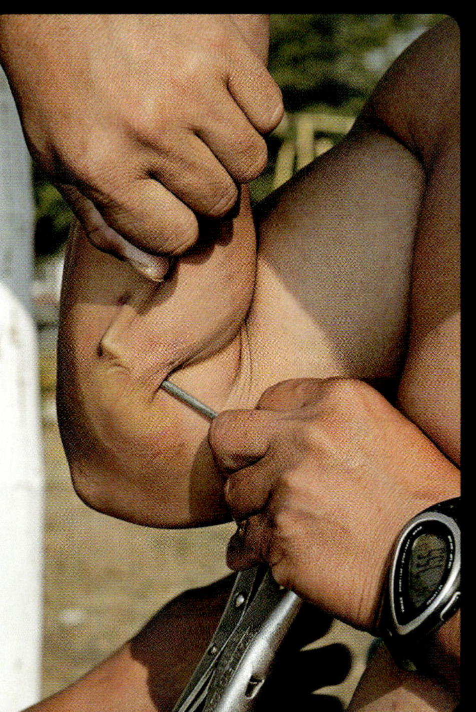

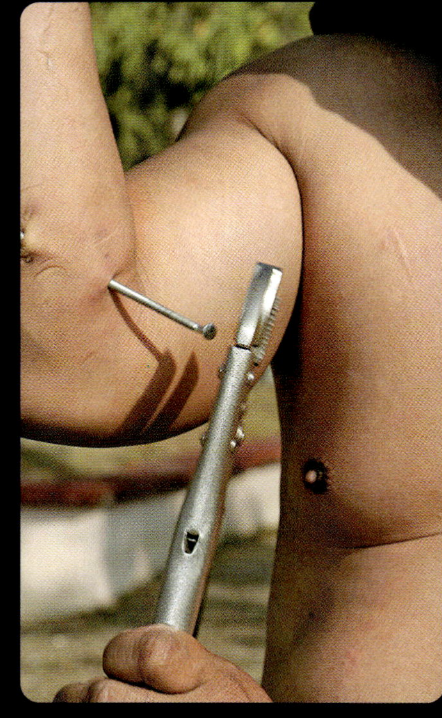

**ABOVE:** Mr. Pain pierces his flesh with large nails in order to attach ropes to his body for this strongman stunt.

**RIGHT:** Caigoy lifts a 180-lb. motorbike using ropes attached to nails that pierce his chest and his forearms.

Attaching a rope to four sharp knives stuck into his stomach, Caigoy drags a 2.8-ton truck nearly 100 feet!

Pain dives into a pile of light bulbs, enduring dozens of sharp glass shards in his back.

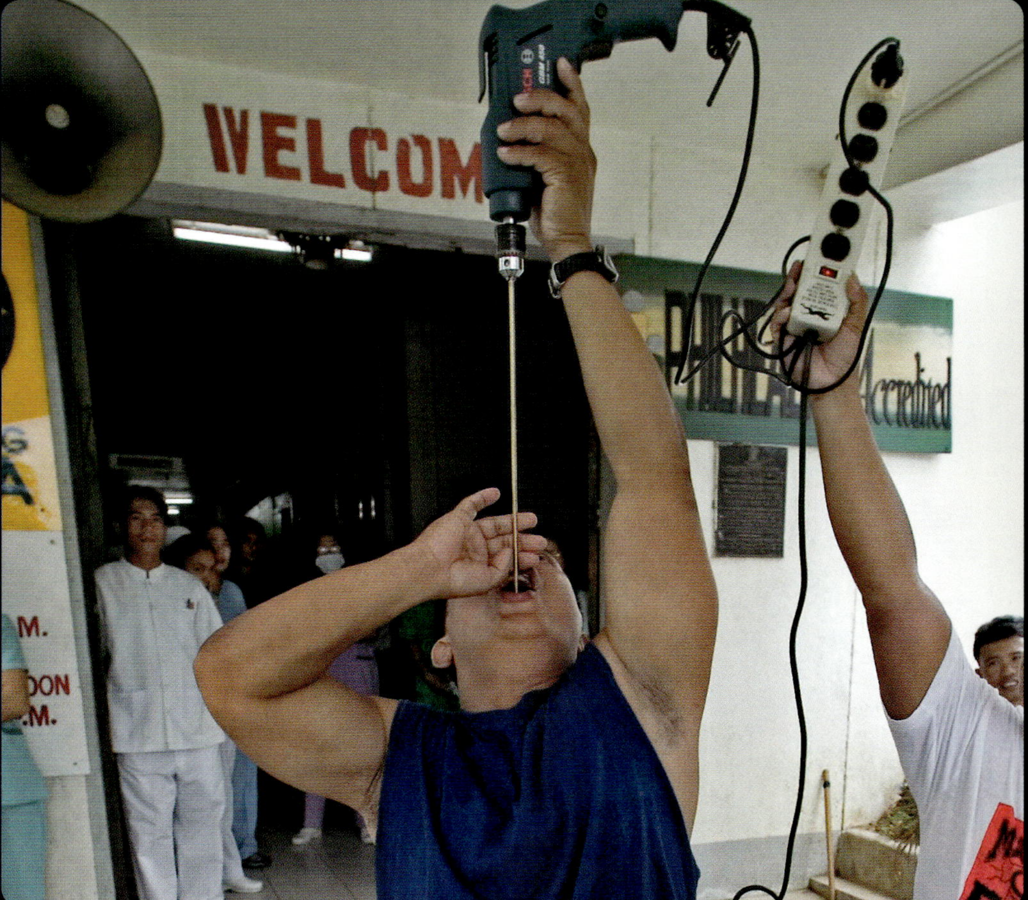

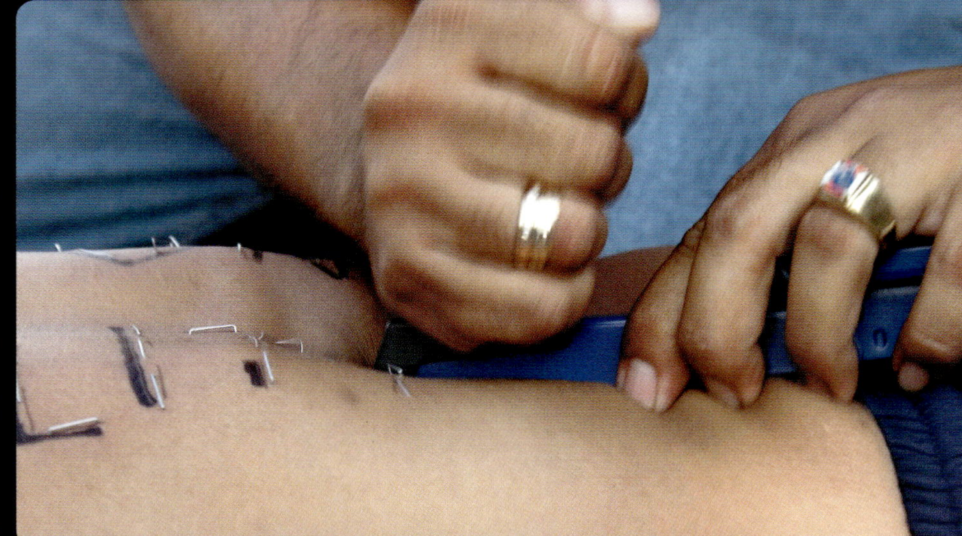

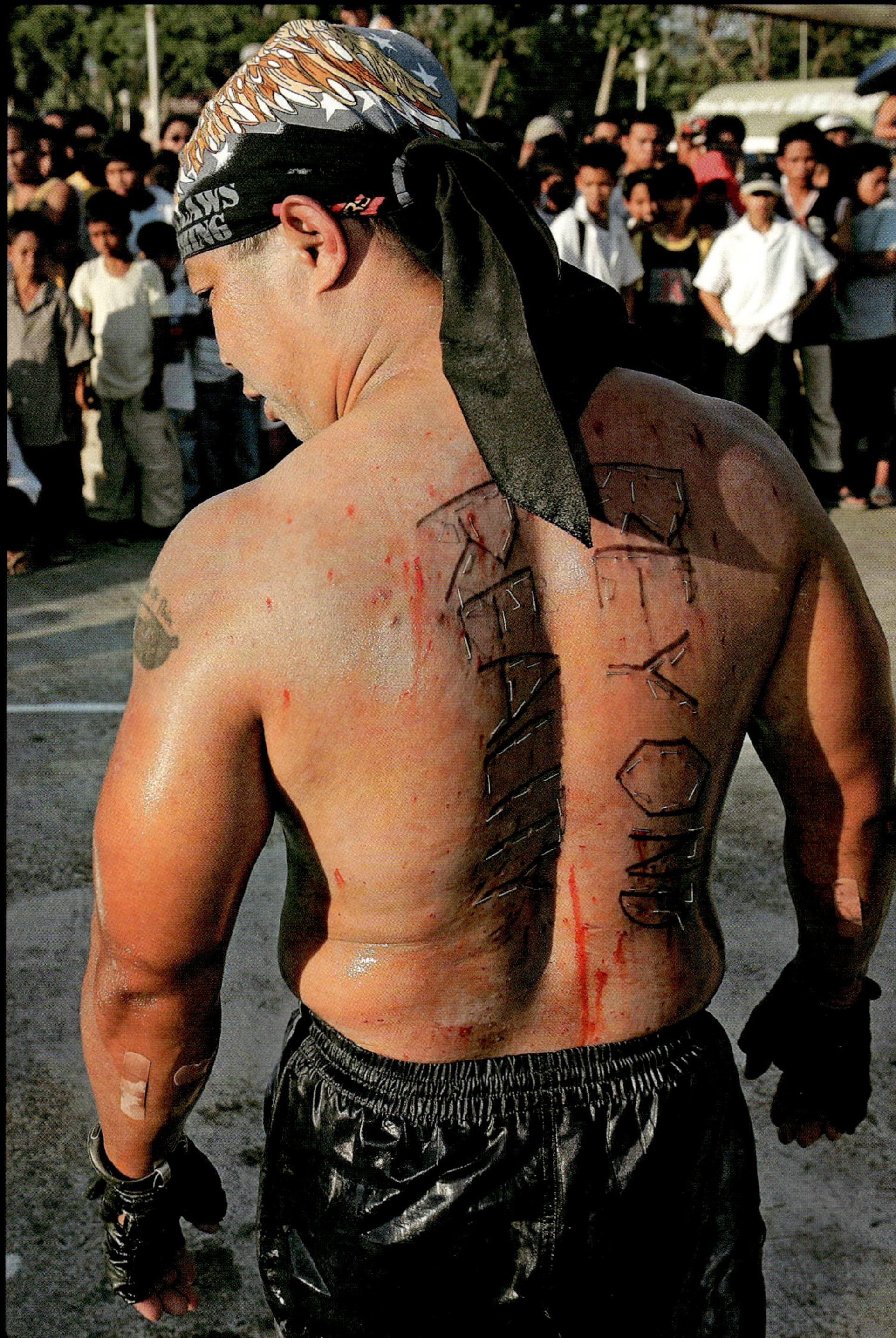


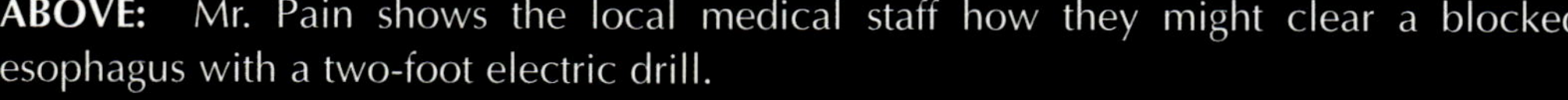

**ABOVE:** Mr. Pain shows the local medical staff how they might clear a blocked esophagus with a two-foot electric drill.

**RIGHT:** Following a body drop during which he smashed 200 fluorescent light bulbs with his back (far bottom right), Caigoy shows off the words "Beyond Reality", which an assistant has driven into his back with a staple gun! Nearly 100 staples were required to finish the temporary tattoo.

# Hard Swallow

HOLLYWOOD, CALIFORNIA

Sword swallower Count Desmond performs an incredibly dangerous stunt never before attempted – simultaneously swallowing 15 coat hangers. Even the slightest slip can cause serious injury and because there are so many sharp ends, the hangers are much more difficult to control than a single sword. The stunt was filmed on the set of an ABC-TV reality show.

# William Tell

SEATTLE, WASHINGTON

Tygerr Recchia is an unflinchingly brave human target for archer Bob Markworth, who recreates the legend of William Tell for my camera. The incredibly steady archery champion uses a crossbow that is easily powerful enough to kill the apple of his eye in a heartbeat, but instead he splits the apple on her head. The couple has performed this stunt thousands of time in more than 50 countries around the world.

# Fancy Footwork

BRANSON, MISSOURI

Claudia Guglielmo is dubbed 'Wonder Woman' for her incredible acts of balance and precision on the sideshow stage. After climbing the steps on one hand, she shoots a bow and arrow upside-down with her feet, hitting her target with unerring aim!

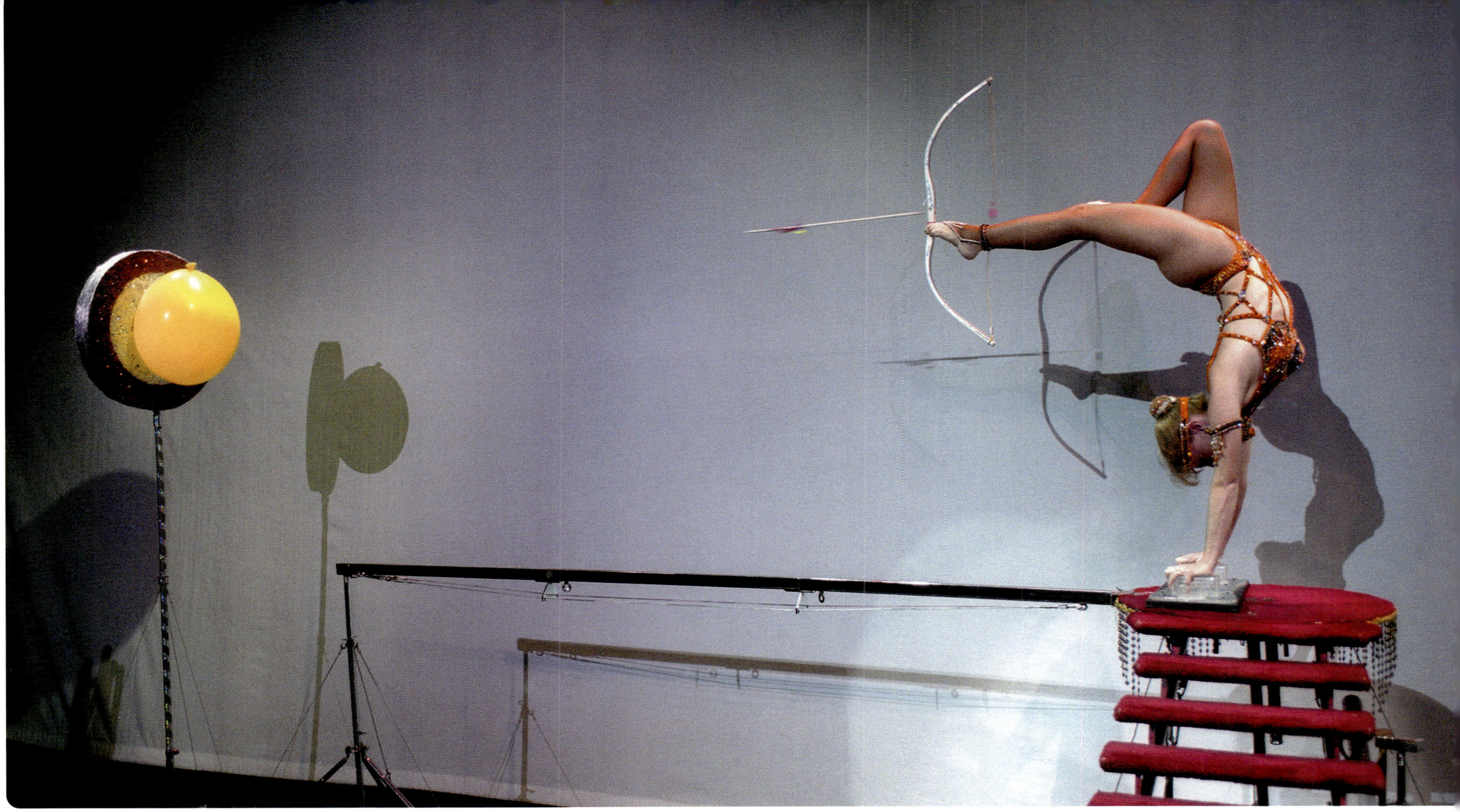

# Got A Light?

SAN FRANCISCO, CALIFORNIA

David Warren, aka 'Flamo Le Grande', is an old-fashioned kind of guy who still lights cigarettes for women. Only, he lights them with his tongue! David is a professional "pyrogenist" or, as they used to call them in the carnival sideshows, a fire-eater. He's also a human barbecue lighter.

# Brotherly Love

GRANGER, INDIANA

John Richmond professes to have shot his brother Ken over 100 times; either in the chest, face, or on top of his head. This time, the two brothers decide to give it a try from a distance of 25 feet with Ken holding a watermelon on top of his head. A deviation of just 1/4" in the marksman's aim will mean certain death for his brother. I use a special Hulcher camera that shoots 65 frames per second to catch the bullet just as it pulverizes its' target.

# BULLET PROOF

FAYETTEVILLE, NORTH CAROLINA

Former military man Jonathan Keith Idema, head of Special Ops Expo and Idema Combat Systems, demonstrates the incredible 'second chance' bulletproof vest by shooting himself in the stomach with a .44 magnum bullet! The red liquid is just fruit punch from a bag that Idema tied to his stomach for dramatic effect. The .44 magnum, Dirty Harry's favorite piece, is the world's most powerful handgun, and though it lodges into the vest's first layer, it still packs a tremendous wallop. But Idema, sore and dazed, still comes back for more, deciding to shoot himself again just a few minutes later. I shot this with a 65 frame-per-second Hulcher camera, capturing more than twice as many frames as a standard motion picture camera — in order to catch the exact instant of impact.

Idema went on to achieve a certain measure of infamy in 2004 by being arrested with two other Americans in Afghanistan, for allegedly posing as American agents running their own private prison. Police found prisoners hanging from their feet. He was sentenced to ten years in an Afghan prison.

# ABS OF STEEL

WILSONVILLE, ALABAMA

Here's an ab workout that won't catch on. Strongman Tom Owen lets a truck packed with 20 kids, weighing an estimated 6,500 pounds, drive over his stomach! While many assume that this stunt is accomplished by moving the truck fast enough to avoid loading its full weight on its target, Owen allowed the truck to stop on top of him for several seconds to ensure I got the shot. Because of the sophistication of my multiple camera setups, the pause was unnecessary but the producers insisted. As a result, though Owen stood and gave the thumbs up shortly after the stunt, he went straight to the Emergency Room with a couple of broken ribs and internal bleeding.

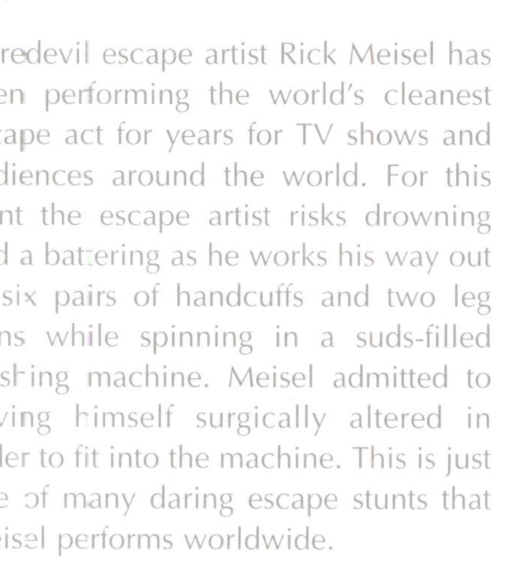

# SPIN CYCLE

ALBUQUERQUE, NEW MEXICO

Daredevil escape artist Rick Meisel has been performing the world's cleanest escape act for years for TV shows and audiences around the world. For this stunt the escape artist risks drowning and a battering as he works his way out of six pairs of handcuffs and two leg irons while spinning in a suds-filled washing machine. Meisel admitted to having himself surgically altered in order to fit into the machine. This is just one of many daring escape stunts that Meisel performs worldwide.

# Karate Head

STOCKTON, CALIFORNIA

In a hard-headed demonstration of strength, skill, and sheer insanity, karate expert Kevin Newton shatters a stack of eight concrete blocks with one tremendous slam of his head, while at the same time smashing another stack with his forearm. An expert in Karate and Tae Kwan Do, Newton is also a pastor who travels the country lecturing students on the dangers of drug and alcohol abuse. He uses demonstrations such as this to warm up his audiences. "It really gets their attention," he says, "and then they're more apt to listen to the message."

# She Bowls 'Em Over!

SHANGHAI, CHINA

In a spectacular exhibition of skill and timing, this Chinese acrobat flips four bowls with her foot into the air and then catches them inside another stack of bowls on her head, all the while balancing precariously on a unicycle high above the ground! And to make this stunt even more amazing, she keeps the unicycle stationary, which — as anyone who's every ridden a bicycle can attest — is incredibly more difficult than keeping her balance while moving.

# GO LONG!

LOS ANGELES, CALIFORNIA

These ex-NFL players take football to great heights in this unusual competition. From a hot-air-balloon tethered more than 75 yards above the football field, a lofty quarterback throws a football to a receiver far down below. The contenders try to catch the ball, which with the acceleration of gravity from 225 feet high, is a high-speed bullet of a pass. The first to succeed gets a check for $1,000, not to mention friction burns on his hands.

# Full Of Hot Air

MONTREAL, CANADA

Entertainer Michael Lauziere stretches the truth about the elasticity of a balloon by blowing up a toy balloon and managing to climb all the way inside. He forms a tight seal around his body, then pulls out a pin and punctures the balloon from within. I shoot the action with a Hulcher camera at 65 frames-per-second, catching the giant balloon in the split-second it pops around him.

# Knight Riders

MONTPELIER, FRANCE

French stuntmen Herve Decalion and Michael Faure use tipping cars instead of horses to re-enact the violent medieval sport of jousting. This hair-raising new twist on the sport requires split-second timing and perfect balance. The match begins with the two cars hitting a specially designed inclined ramp to tip up at a sixty-degree angle as they approach each other at 20 mph. The players climb out the car windows to stand on top of the moving vehicles for battle. The jousters, whose armor is composed of protective suits and hi-tech helmets, are armed with shields and 9-foot bamboo lances. The cars are tightly controlled by highly skilled drivers who must maintain both a steady speed and angle on two wheels for the safety of the combatants. After several passes, Decalion – who has a considerable height advantage – succeeds in knocking Faure from his precarious perch.

# Hitting The Nail On The Head

GRANGER, INDIANA

In one of the wackiest stunts ever, daredevil Ken Richmond allows his brother John to drop a 16-pound bowling ball 27 feet onto a spike-filled board on his head! John drops the ball from a cherry-picker crane. The ball slams into five cement blocks balanced on top of the spiked board and shatters them, slamming the spikes into Ken's head. After the bizarre stunt, Richmond holds a rag to his head to control the flow of blood from his 27 puncture wounds.

# Over Easy

MONTREAL, CANADA

Flipping their way to a new world record, 28 pro skiers perform this breathtaking simultaneous back flip at Bromont Ski Resort. Holding hands, the 24 men and 4 women ski up a steep 6-foot jump ramp marked with their names to keep them lined up properly. Once airborne, and still holding hands, they flip 360-degrees in unison. As they land in a flurry of snow, the 28 skiers raise their arms in triumph. They beat the old record by a wide margin of seven skiers.

KAR
AIR

# Human Bee-ings

DAVIS, CALIFORNIA

Six charming cheerleaders from UC Davis smear themselves with bee bait and form a human pyramid to attract over a million bees for their moment of glory. The attractant, called Essence of Queen Bee, duplicates the scent of the queen bee and brings the drones and workers swarming in the mistaken impression that a new beehive needs forming. First, the girls have their ears and noses stopped up with wax so the swarming bees can't crawl in. Then, when they are in formation, the bees are released from the hive and make a beeline for the pyramid in a dark, buzzing cloud, covering the girls' bodies. For some it is a painful encounter. Several of the girls are stung a number of times. But all courageously hold their position for nearly fifteen minutes, breaking all previous records. The swarm is big enough to earn them a spot in the Guinness Book of World Records.

CLEVELAND, OHIO

Below left, Jim Johnson sets a Guinness world record for the largest Bee Beard. Johnson ties a fertile queen around his neck in a pouch; this attracts 35,000 workers, weighing 10 pounds, to his face. Johnson ties off his pant and shirt cuffs and stuffs cotton up his nose and ears to keep the bees out. The previous bee beard record was 21,000 bees.

Below right, a man in a top hat gives his own queen bee a kiss.

# No Holds Barred

LONG BEACH, CALIFORNIA

Darrin Carter walks from one end of the Villa Riviera to the other on a slack line, 15 floors above the ground, covering a distance of approximately 150 feet! Carter crawled through a window onto the ledge and began his walk, high above downtown Long Beach, with no harness and no safety net. One small slip would have sent him plunging to certain death on the hard street below. This incredible death-defying stunt was filmed for a segment of *Ripley's Believe It or Not!*

# CARS GONE WILD

CHARLOTTE, NORTH CAROLINA

Brian Carson withstands the heat from multiple fire bombs as his car becomes enveloped in flames while jumping over four flatbed trucks at Charlotte Motor Speedway. Fortunately for the nearly roasted Carson, a fire retardant suit and a quick-acting safety crew saves him a trip to the ER.

SPEED SPORT
UNIFORMS
DANGER
STAY

# No Way To Treat A Caddy

CHARLOTTE, NORTH CAROLINA

Daredevil Brian Carson attempts to leap his 1986 Cadillac Seville over four flatbed trucks parked end-to-end, and through four walls of flame. He doesn't quite make it and ends up landing on top of one of my cameras. Luckily, I'm operating it remotely. Carson miraculously walks away unscathed, but the camera is DOA. I'm able to extract the film from the smashed camera to discover this picture of him strapped inside the car with his arms folded, seemingly waiting to crash. The center shot on the far right shows the car taking out the camera.

# Topsy Turvy

CHARLOTTE, NORTH CAROLINA

Daredevil Brian Carson is attempting this corkscrew stunt for the first time, and the result isn't pretty. Carson races his car at 70 mph up a ramp that is designed to spiral the vehicle through the air like a football through a flaming pyre, before landing wheels down, on a line of parked cars. Unfortunately after 150 feet of twisting in the wind up to four stories high, Carson's car drops like a rock, upside-down, onto its top. Once again, amazingly, Carson walks away unharmed.

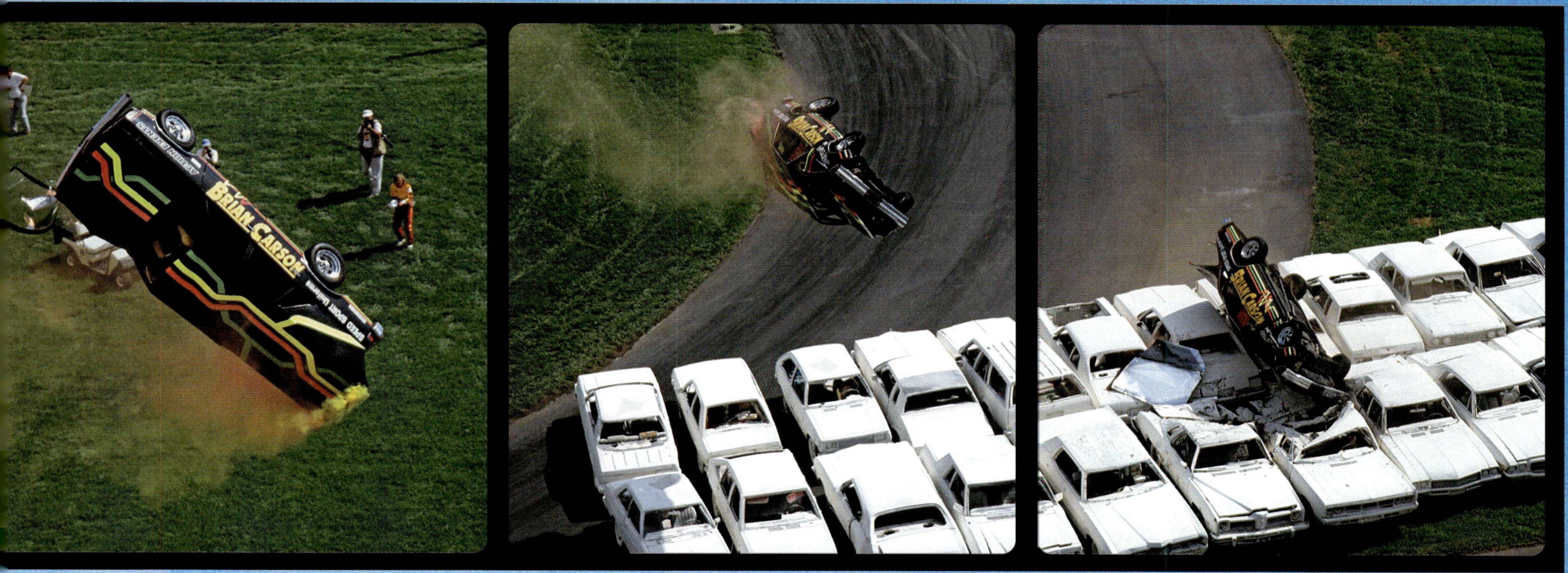
BRIAN CARSON

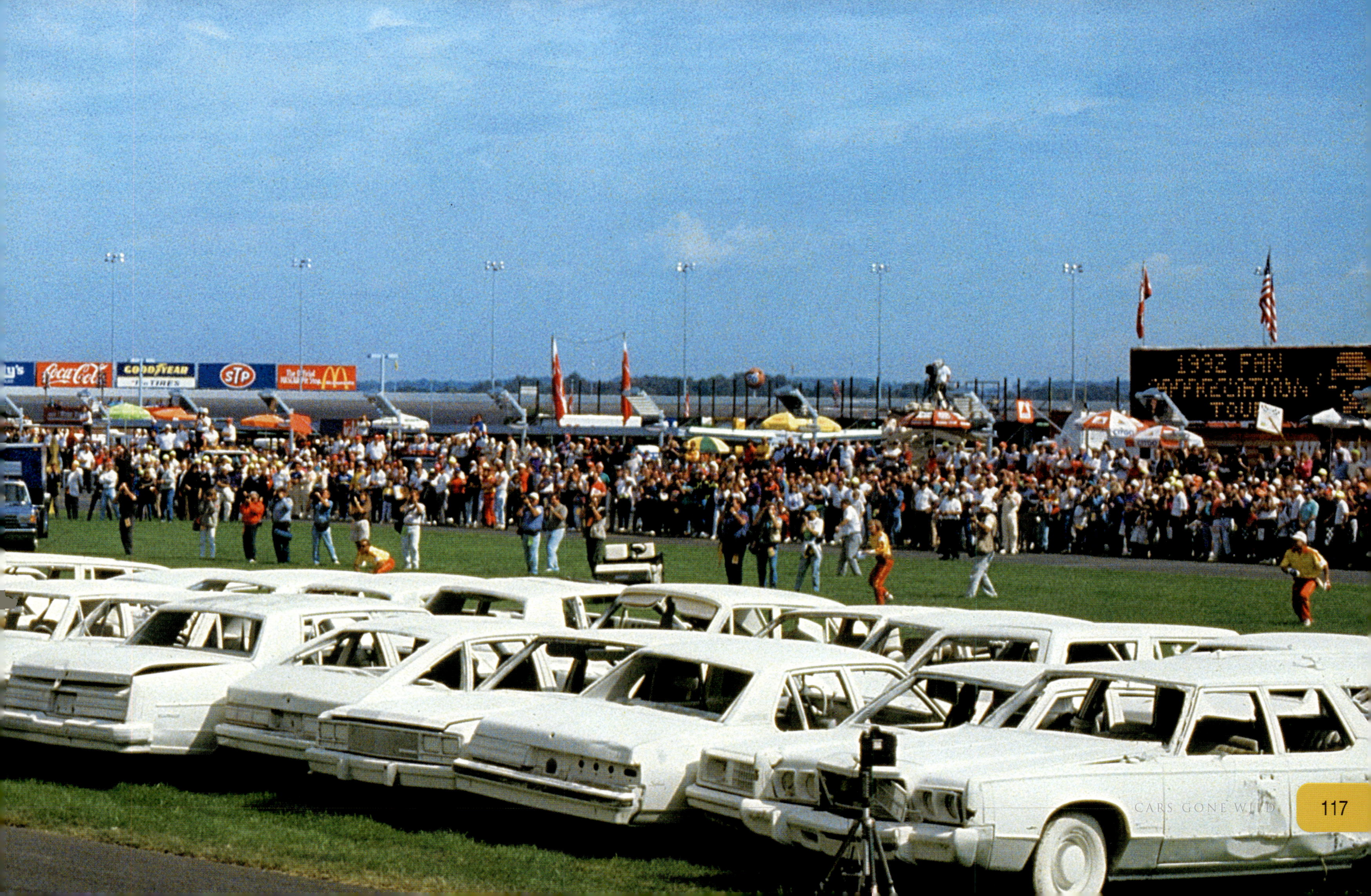
Coca-Cola
GOODYEAR
STP
1992 FAN

# Falling Star

SAN DIEGO, CALIFORNIA

Brian Carson performs a stunt where it's hard to miss his target. The cars drops 180 feet straight down into a massive explosion! Hoisted by crane to his start position, high above the ground at Jack Murphy Stadium, using a pile of cars to cushion his fall, Carson begins his terrifying plunge with an explosion that turns his car into a spark-shooting comet. He streaks toward the waiting cars, which explode in a giant fireball on contact. The stadium crowd holds its' breath as rescuers run onto the field to extinguish the flames. But the daredevil, protected by a built-in cage and a 3-layered flame-retardant suit, emerges unhurt from the wreck with a new record under his belt.

# Shaken Not Stirred

VALBERG, FRANCE

In a death-defying leap, stuntman Dominique Julienne flies his tiny yellow Fiat off the giant Olympic ski jump in Valberg, France and soars through the air at 60 mph. A breakaway cable hooked to the car's front bumper jerks the car's nose up, sending Julienne's car spinning head-over-heels, or trunk-over-hood, through space. For several heart-stopping seconds, he tumbles wildly before landing on his target, a pile of fall-breaking boxes. As Julienne touches down, his dad, stunt legend Remy Julienne — creator of many of the James Bond movie stunts — throws up his arms in celebration. Shot for *World's Greatest Stunts II*, the driver, safe and sound, skis the car the rest of the way down the slope.

# BLACK-AND-WHITE IN FLIGHT

ORLANDO, FLORIDA

Stuntman Mark Hagar's police car flies high in a fiery jump during a three-day crash fest at an airport near Orlando. Hager, a professional stuntman for almost two decades, has coordinated and performed more than 700 car stunts nationwide, including his 1995 record-breaking 213-foot bus jump at a Charlotte Motor Speedway NASCAR event. He currently holds four world records.

# BLIND FAITH

BENSON, ARIZONA

Joe Skorpen takes off his stunt coordinator hat during the filming of *I Dare You: The Ultimate Challenge* to get behind the wheel and race a Z28 Camaro toward the side of a speeding freight train at 50 mph. There is only one flatbed in the train, creating just a momentary gap between the massive cars for Skorpen to try to jump through. If he misses, he'll smash head-on into a steel freight car. As the train approaches, and his safety crew flags him on, Skorpen guns the Camaro and takes off. When he hits the ramp at speed, all he can see is the broadside of the train. A split-second later, he spots flames and knows that he's looking at a firebomb on the flatbed, telling him he's hit his mark. Skorpen soars through the flames to strike the road hard but safely on the other side of the tracks.

RAIL
CROS

# TRAINED FOR DISASTER

BENSON, ARIZONA

Hollywood stuntman Chuck Borden straps himself into a 4-wheel-drive 1973 International Harvester Scout with the intention of driving head-on into a train for the TV show *I Dare You.* The train is equipped with a pipe ramp that juts from the front of the engine so as the two vehicles meet, Borden's truck will go up the ramp and jump the speeding train with a corkscrew spin. If all goes well, he'll land on the ground beside the tracks. The stunt has never been attempted by anyone before, so nerves are on edge as Borden barrels down a railroad track at 45 mph, straight toward the approaching million-pound freight train. Without an escape route, everything must go perfectly. Unfortunately, it doesn't: Borden hits the pipe ramp, and a giant explosion of pyro bombs goes off as intended. But before he can fully launch, the ramp breaks as shown at bottom left. Borden's truck crashes into the locomotive dead-on! The steel-grinding impact sends the near-totaled truck spinning and reeling into the ground. Amazingly, Borden walks away from the wreckage! A failed attempt? Not according to Borden: "Hey, anytime you can walk away from a mid-air crash with an oncoming freight train, I guess you can call that a successful stunt!"

3134
SCRX

# CRISS-CROSS

KINGMAN, ARIZONA

Stunt drivers Spanky Spangler and Tommy 'Trouble' McTuage attempt an over-under criss-cross double jump. This is an especially dangerous stunt because two drivers are airborne in the same vertical space at the same time, so if anything goes wrong, two lives will be lost. Spangler, in a yellow Cutlass and McTauge in a red Grand Prix, race down a 600-foot runway at exactly 65 mph. They jump their cars simultaneously, but Spangler's ramp is five feet higher than McTauge's, intended to launch Spangler over and above the other car. The men criss-cross in mid-air, Spangler above McTauge, through a massive explosive fireball. To make matters worse, instead of a soft landing pad, or even a flat one, they both fly more than 100 feet into a bunch of lined-up cars. "I did a big header right into the cars," Spangler says, a bit shaken. "There weren't enough out there to buffer me completely, so I went off and hit ground. What a ride!"

I DARE YOU!

# Rocket Across The Rio Grande

SANTA FE, NEW MEXICO

Stuntman Spanky Spangler is blasted in a rocket-powered truck across the Rio Grande River at a height of 25 feet. The truck flies for 150 feet before crash-landing into a sacred Indian burial ground, on the far shore. The truck is destroyed but the Native American spirits must be on Spangler's side, because he escapes without injury within 10 feet of his intended landing spot. Ky 'Rocket Man' Michaelson designed the rocket truck for an airing of GRB Entertainment's *World's Greatest Stunts* tv special.

## TRASH LANDING!

CHARLOTTE, NORTH CAROLINA

Stuntman Dennis Pinto flies a heavy trash collector 50 feet through the air at 65 mph to crash land in an explosive fireball onto a double row of cars. Pinto emerged unharmed from the pileup as clean as a whistle, although the garbage truck was a little worse for wear.

HOWARD
SANITATION
EXPRESS
HARLOT

HOWARD
SANITATION
EXPRESS

# Sky Crash!

HOUSTON, TEXAS

Before a stunned crowd of 55,000 at the Astrodome, Spanky Spangler stages a mid-air collision into another car driven by his friend and fellow stuntman Randy Hill. Both stuntmen are strapped in their cars with special crash protectors built in, but with two cars colliding head-on at 50 mph each, their crash is the equivalent of hitting a brick wall at 120 mph! Despite the numbing impact, both human crash dummies walk away uninjured. "A lot of people were saying my body wouldn't be able to take the impact, that my heart would stop," says Spangler. "Of course, being in mid-air absorbs some of the shock, because the cars have another direction to go in — down." A 20-year veteran of stunt driving, Spangler spent three years preparing for this stunt, carefully examining the wrecks of every car he crashed, in order to log speeds, jump heights, and impact damage. The successful stunt was the pinnacle of the two men's careers.

And then, more then a decade later…

LA
AJFoyt
RANDY
HILL
AJFoyt
J-P
SPANKY
SPANGLER

SPANKY
RANDY

Randy Hill and Spanky Spangler at the Houston Astrodome in 1981.

# REQUIEM FOR A STUNTMAN

SAN ANTONIO, TEXAS

November 13, 1993. I started the day in Florida attending a family event. My assistant, Terry Caccia, started his in Los Angeles, packing all of my cameras and equipment into cases. Later that day, we both boarded planes heading to Texas, and met up at the Alamodome in the late afternoon. We spent the next few hours setting up 15 cameras in anticipation of yet a third take of one of the most awesome stunts I had ever shot; Spanky and Randy's Sky Crash. It had been twelve years since the last one at the Houston Astrodome, but I still remembered the rush of seeing two cars crash head-on at 50 mph into an explosion of steel and glass. Ironically, Hill had retired from performing stunts, but had come back for one more show which he dedicated to the memory of his brother Rodney, a fellow stuntman who had been killed in a stunt three years earlier. Expecting another spectacular crash, I wanted to set up even more cameras than I had on the last two, covering the ceiling looking down, the press box, the floor, inside the car...every angle possible. Nothing could have prepared me for the tragic outcome of this picture — the moment of death, shown so vividly. As the cameras fire, I'm shooting tight on Hill's car, and it's immediately evident that something has gone terribly wrong. In front of 15,000 shocked spectators, the two souped-up Chevys careen toward each other, but instead of colliding straight-on as planned, Spangler's car shears the top of Hill's vehicle, killing him instantly. "Randy came off the ramp a little slow and his car didn't come up high enough to meet me head-on. He never had a chance," said a grief-stricken Spangler. "I loved Randy," he said. "His death is very hard for me to take."

**Dennis Madalone**, a stuntman and stunt coordinator, parlayed a one-day gig on *Star Trek: The Next Generation* into a 14-year stint as the Stunt Coordinator for *Star Trek: Next Generation*, *Star Trek: Deep Space 9*, and *Star Trek: Voyager*, sometimes working on two shows at once. He has since worked on many other shows, including four years stunt coordinating *Without a Trace* and the feature film *Poor Things* starring Shirley MacLaine and Olympia Dukakis. He is also known for his 2005 patriotic song and music video, *America We Stand as One*, which became an Internet phenomenon.

---

**Q: As a stunt person, you get into the same make-up as the actors, right? So, you essentially look like the actor in order to play their double. What is that like?**

A: I've doubled people on all three Star Trek series. But I also played characters myself, many times with dialogue, and also played hundreds of Klingons and Jemadars, with five pounds of rubber on my face and rubber wetsuits even when it was 100 degrees. I just come running in as a Klingon and get killed within two seconds and fans freeze-frame and look at my nose, and they know who I am. I was always interested in doing stunts, but I was also a good actor. It's great when a producer can hire you to do a couple lines of dialogue and do the stunt as well.

**Q: Can you talk a little bit about air rams?**

A: I hold the world record on air rams that I set on the *Guinness Book of World Records* show, years ago, where I went 28 feet 7 inches to my back on concrete. An air ram is a flat device that's 2 feet by 3, and only 7 or 8 inches tall. It opens up with hydraulics like a diving board. As it opens, it flips you and propels you. That device is really my forté, because I used it a lot on an '80s TV series called the *Greatest American Hero*. I loved it, because I would run and hit the air ram, and it sent me flying into anything and everything.

**Q: What about actors that do their own stunts? Do you know any famous actors that like to do their own stunts or that actually insist on doing them?**

A: Robert Conrad from *Baa Baa Black Sheep* and *Wild Wild West* always loved doing his own stunts; he was really super handy. Burt Reynolds started as a stuntman, and then started to star in films too. He was famous for always eating the ground and the camera seeing his face. He lived with Hal Needham, a famous stuntman. But when it comes down to something dangerous, like flipping a car, or high falls, or fire gags, the actors know when to sit down and let their buddies do it.

**Q: When you stage a fight, what do you do in order to make it seem real?**

A: All stunt coordinators have different styles. I was trained by Paul Stader - he was kind of a boxer and streetfighter, and that's the style I got. When I put a fight together, I'm trying to utilize the environment I'm in, whether that's a room or a roof or a street. It makes the fight much more realistic than just throwing punches back and forth.

**Q: When punches are thrown or when you see contact between two people, how hard are they hitting?**

A: All the punches to the face are all misses. Right camera angles make them look like hits. Of course, with the sound effects, it makes it sound like we've punched somebody in the face. But when it come to flipping people to the ground or throwing people onto tables, that's pretty realistic. We also take stomach punches, where you make a little contact but not too much. A lot of it is adding the sound effects to make it sound real, which will make it look real too.

**Q: What about a show like Fear Factor? I'm sure there's a stunt coordinator on that show. Are the stunts that they do as dangerous as they look?**

A: At first I wasn't comfortable with that show, since it uses regular people doing dangerous stunts. But the bottom line is, if you have great stunt coordinators and great riggers, you can do a lot of things with people that don't have knowledge of stunts. It is also important though, that they pick healthy people. As you get older and more out of shape, it gets harder to do stunts. Stuntmen have to stay in good shape, no matter what.

INTERVIEW

**Joe Skorpen** is a stunt coordinator for television and movies. He was essentially trained on the job, but his background is in fire rescue and martial arts. He started by working on shows during his time off from fire-fighting. Skorpen oversees the safety parameters on a stunt, from determining whether or not a stunt can be done safely, to the obligatory safety meeting immediately before its performance - the last of many meetings that go into keeping stunts safe. Skorpen spends months in planning before a stunt ever makes it to set.

**Q: You were the stunt coordinator on the show *I Dare You.* Can you talk about how you would prepare for a complex stunt?**

A: I got a proposal for a guy to bungee jump from a flying helicopter while another helicopter flew beneath it. I knew the FAA would never approve it. But I knew that if we put one of these helicopters on the ground, and then hovered one over it, we had a good shot at getting that approved. The FAA has no jurisdiction on aircraft on the ground. Also, in that way, I could increase the distance between the performer and the blades by putting a camera on the ground beneath the helicopter that's on the ground and filming through the rotating blades. So it'll look really great, it will be a better shot and we have a chance of getting it approved. I'm the only one in the business that I know of, that can actually perform trajectory calculations on a calculator using physics before we do the stunt.

**Q: As far as timing goes for these stunts, it's pretty much down to seconds or even hundredths of a second, right?**

A: It is, but if you can maintain constant speeds during practice and constant accelerations during practice, you can calculate it.

**Q: Can you speak about the difference between stuntmen and daredevils, and why there might be what you would call contention between stuntmen who some people call daredevils?**

A: Stuntmen need to be able to do something over and over again, during several takes. Daredevils do more live shows, so they do it once and go home. There's a big difference in performance and approach to the stunt – and, I personally think, a safety difference too.

**Q: You did a stunt in front of hundreds of thousands of dollars worth of TV cameras, but Jeff got the only image of that...**

A: There were a few stunts, one of which was my train stunt, where the best shot came from Jeff. But, for this limo stunt, the only shot came from Jeff. The gag consisted of a limo popped into the air and before it came down, another car would drive beneath it. The guy that did the stunt also did pyrotechnics - he set up gas bombs in a circle all around the limos. The bombs fired off as the limousine lifted off the ground, and he drove beneath it. Everything was completely whited out [from the bright light of the fires,] and people were saying that it was a staged fake stunt. Without Jeff's photographs of the car going up and the stunt car traveling beneath it, we would have never been able to prove that it was real.

**Q: Are there any famous actors you know that came from stunts? And do you have any favorite actors to work with?**

A: Some actors are allowed to do some stunts, but no one does all their own stunts because the insurance companies would never allow it. A lot of actors get away with claiming that they do their own stunts, because a stuntman wants to be allowed to keep doubling an actor. Stuntmen just understand that it's our job to be in the background. As for actors that started as stuntmen, Burt Reynolds was a stuntman first.

**Q: Do you have any funny or unusual anecdotes about actors that you've worked with that have done their own stunts?**

A: I was working with Dennis Hopper on a film – I believe it was *Tycus* – and he was in a scene where he is shot, and he needed to fall down. Dennis just decided to fall on the hard concrete right there on the set. I'm standing there with a three-inch thick pad, and I saw him start to fall down, and when he was about a foot from the ground, I just slid it from where I was standing right along the floor. It landed perfectly right underneath him, just as he made contact. He looked at me, the director looked at me, and the crew applauded. Dennis stood up, came over to shake my hand, and said, "Man that was pretty quick."

# SPANGLER
INTERVIEW

**Spanky Spangler** is a stuntman recognized by the Stuntmen Hall of Fame for his incredible body of work, which includes more than 22,000 stunts. He began performing stunts in films at 12 and as a teenager, trained at jump school. One of the youngest Green Berets in history, he has set 22 world records. He also holds the distinction of having September 13th named "Spanky Spangler Day" after him by the Governor of Arizona.

**Q: What do you consider your most spectacular stunt?**

A: It's hard to say. I jumped a car 328 feet. I jumped a car 232 feet over water. I jumped out of a helicopter onto a speeding truck going 45 miles an hour, and I jumped out of a helicopter and landed in the back of the tractor-trailer rig 75 feet below.

**Q: At 12, I'm sure you needed permission or help to get started performing stunts. How did your family play a role in that?**

A: My father died when I was four years old, and my mother raised me, so I was kind of on my own. I did what I wanted to do. I was at a studio and I was doubling for a kid. I jumped out of a wagon and went into the bushes and they paid me 15 dollars. I thought all the kids did that at that age. When I first started, stuntmen weren't very popular, because they weren't allowed to say they did stunts for anybody; the actors got all the credit.

**Q: Did your mom support you?**

A: Yes. Well, no parent wants you to do it, but that's where I'm gifted. I've done shows in front of 60,000 people in a packed house at the Astrodome.

**Q: Let's talk a little bit about your name. Is there a story behind it?**

A: It's a nickname I got when I was a little kid, and it just kind of stuck. When you get into entertainment, you want to be a little different, and it was catchy.

**Q: Your partner Randy Hill came out of retirement in 1994 to redo the sky-crash stunt, in Texas, which Jeff shot, and the result was tragic...**

A: I don't like to do stunts with other people because of this. Randy had problems with his car at the bottom of the ramp, and he lost his speed, and we can never really find out exactly what happened. He got killed in that accident. I didn't want to do that stunt. I was coming off an injury. Randy really wanted to do it one more time, so he put it together himself. When we did our final approach, he dropped short. I was in the apex of the jump, where we were supposed to hit, but his car never quite made it. I quit for a year after that. He wasn't only a stunt friend of mine. Losing him was like losing my right arm. He was one of my best friends, and there's not a day that goes by that I don't think about it. But it's a tough business, and it's not for everybody. I helped a lot of guys get into the business and I try to give them all the calculations and to help everybody as much as I can because I don't want to see anybody get hurt. I tip my hat to anybody who puts on a helmet and tries to do what we do, but it's very dangerous.

**Q: What kind of personality do you think it takes to get into doing this type of work?**

A: It's very challenging and you have to be very confident in what you do. In a movie I jumped a car into 232 feet of water, and the car got stuck upside down. I had oxygen in the car but I lost my oxygen and my front window pushed in, so I didn't have any oxygen. I was upside down, it was dark, and my car was stuck. I had to slow my body down, so my movements wouldn't use up so much oxygen. I held my breath for two-and-a-half minutes until the divers got to me. I was able to signal to them with my hands that I was out of oxygen, and they pried the door open. It was at a place called Firebird Lake, in Arizona, for an NBC television show called *Games People Play*. So I had NBC there with cameras and helicopters, and I was down in the water for three minutes and eighteen seconds. It was a very tough stunt. Two guys did it in Europe before I tried it, and they both got killed. They don't even put the stunt in the *Guinness Book of World* Records anymore, because they don't want people to try it.

**Gary R. Benz**, President and CEO of GRB Entertainment, is a leading Hollywood producer of reality-television programming. He was also business partner and close friend to legendary stuntman Dar Robinson, before Robinson's tragic death while performing a routine motorcycle stunt in 1986. Benz has produced hours of action-themed reality programming, including *Live: The World's Greatest Stunts* and *The World's Most Dangerous Stunts*. In 1987, Benz produced *The Ultimate Stuntman: A Tribute to Dar Robinson* featuring Chuck Norris and Mel Gibson. Nobody knows more about producing stunt shows for television than Benz, so after a five-year hiatus from the genre, he is producing a new stunt-based series.

**Q: How did you get into the business?**

A: I think it was 1979; I met Dar Robertson when I went down to Mexico City for a thrill show. Dar was the premiere act. When I met him, he was very charismatic and fun as hell and just a wonderful guy – loved women you know, loved jokes but also was enormously talented. We became business partners.

**Q: Can you tell me why so many in the stunt business see Dar as the world's best stuntman, ever?**

A: Dar had a phenomenal inner ear. You could spin him around, and he wouldn't get disoriented. Also, he wasn't that old breed of stuntman who would pick himself up after a stunt, dust himself off and say, "Oh, I only broke a couple of ribs." He was known as a stunt scientist, because he would test things ahead of time. He would use computers to model and plan and conceive stunts. He raised the safety bar, and he never broke a bone in his life. It's unbelievable: the guy had 33 world records and world firsts and never broke a bone. He did not like pain at all, and so he would think everything through and be very careful. Ironically, he lost his life on a movie set not even doing a stunt. It's irony at its most tragic.

**Q: I've heard a lot of people say that the big contention between daredevils and stunt people is that some think that daredevils take stunts too lightly.**

A: To be a top Hollywood stunt person, you have to be trained in a lot of different disciplines. Everyday, you get a different assignment. Daredevils look to do a big trick. They set up a ramp where a car is gonna fly 100 feet, and then they try to figure out what to crash it into. They don't have the money to plan and check their stunts.

**Q: And, stuntmen aren't as visible publicly...**

A: Yeah. On camera, they have wigs and makeup on. They don't want the glory. Dar was one of the few who actually played in both worlds, and he liked that, because – quite honestly – he was a bit of a ham.

**Q: Why is it that Evel Knievel is such a household name?**

A: Because he was a brilliant promoter. You see a guy named Evel talking, and he's wearing a flamboyant red-white-and-blue leather jumpsuit, and he's saying, "Ok, I broke all those bones, but I'm coming back, and I'm gonna do it again in three months, so come on out and watch me." And, it's different: He did it big.

**Q: So, let's say that you have a skill, whether it's racing or gymnastics, and you want to get into the business. Where would you start?**

A: It's pretty tough. Usually, when somebody wants to break into the business, they come out here to Hollywood, and they start calling all the stunt organizations to befriend someone. Many will work for free. The top 100 stunt guys make a really good living.

**Q: Dar's project was your first project for GRB Entertainment?**

A: I was going to do a tribute to Dar, because, even though we eventually went our own ways business-wise, I loved him dearly. I was initially just going to do it for his friends and family, but I went to ABC, and they said, "Hey, if you get Burt Reynolds and Mel Gibson, and all the clips from *That's Incredible* that you did, and all the movies he did, and put it all together, then we'll buy a one-hour tribute special." It did very, very well. I actually got a lot of positive feedback from many people who knew Dar who had seen it.

**Q: So, the project remained a genuine tribute to Dar, despite the wider audience?**

A: Yeah... I hired a wonderful writer who spent a lot of time with me, because I was so familiar with Dar and his body of work. We dove into it and spent all that time just trying to distill the essence of who Dar was. It was a labor of love.

**Reckless Rex Phelps** is a daredevil who started riding motorcycles when he was just 10 years old. Six years later he jumped 10 Chevy trucks on a 504 Honda road bike at a Montana county fair. In the '70s he was one of the first stuntmen ever to perform a back-flip on a motorcycle. In 1987 Phelps was seriously injured in a crash. After a nine-year jumping hiatus, he returned to the sport and now performs at charity events across the United States. Al's Cycle, in Hamilton, Montana, has loaned Rex many of the motorcycles he has used in his stunts.

**Q: When did you first hear of Evel Knievel?**

A: I saw him on TV: He was in a big crash 50 miles from my house. It was one of his first jumps, and my step-dad and I watched him crash. I'd never seen anything like it in my life. I remember thinking that Superman was trying to ride a motorcycle and that he should stick to flying, because he was crashing the motorcycle really bad. It was actually a terrible crash and my step-dad yelled at me and said, "You better not ever try anything like that."

**Q: How did you end up meeting Evel and working with him?**

A: After the '76 jump, I jumped 12 trucks, in Helena, Montana, and Evel called me up. He asked me why I was jumping so far and told me I was going to kill myself. In 1979, a friend introduced me to Evel, and we talked about doing stunts together and going to Japan. But I got busted up jumping on a drag strip in '82. He called me up after that crash as well, and told me to get the pins out of my shoulder. He wanted to take me to Huntington, West Virginia to do flips. We did a show there, and I crashed twice the first night. I pulled off the stage and smashed a bike into a wall, and he loved it.

**Q: Did Evel jump at the shows you did together?**

A: The whole time I was with Evel, he never did ride; he was already retired in '82. In the '80s, he'd already been through it all. Instead, he was doing these really beautiful paintings.

**Q: You have injured yourself a lot in the course of your career. You had a particularly bad accident in Seattle in '87...**

A: I've been in about 20 bad crashes. There was one in which I hit the side of the tank. I knew I shouldn't have jumped that night. It was foggy at Oakland stadium. I looked up at the lights, and I could see the fog misting down. Everybody was worried about me jumping, but they had paid me ten grand in advance to make sure I was going to do it. When I got to the top of the ramp, the bike slipped 6 inches to one side, which took me clear out of the tank, to the side, and I looked down at the plywood on the stadium floor, which they had laid out to protect the baseball field. I knew I was doomed. I looked for the tank and tried to get to the tank as best I could, but I ended up hitting the edge of it, and the bike ended up on the ground. I shattered my leg and smacked my head and ended up in the hospital for a year.

**Q: How long did it take for you to walk, never mind jump, again?**

A: Actually, it was 9 years before I jumped again. I was all busted up lying in one bed in my house, and my son was lying in another, almost dying from drinking some bad water, and my wife walked in and said, "You have to promise to never jump again or our marriage is over." So I promised her that I would never jump again. Nine years later, we were sitting at home, and I ended up walking out to my van and leaving. I went over to Hamilton, Montana and I called up Jeff Werner and Bill Graham and asked if they could help me. I wanted to do a stunt for Feed the Children, and they came over and filmed it. I did the backwards ride several times, and that was the beginning. I had a brace on my leg for a long time, a big plastic thing which came up to my knee.

**Q: When you first saw Evel jump, your stepfather warned you to never get into anything like that. How do you feel about your kids getting into what you do?**

A: They all ride, and we all have motorcycles from Al's, but none of them are daredevils. They've seen their dad come home busted up a lot, and they never were interested in it at all, which is a big relief. Now, they're too old. You have to start when you're a little kid to really make something out of it.

**Q: Do you have any words of wisdom or words of advice for the young kids who are out there doing these things, like extreme sports and riding dirt bikes and pushing the limits, the way you've been doing your entire life?**

A: I can't say anything to those guys. They're awesome, and they're crazier than I am.

# PLANTICO

INTERVIEW

**Nick Plantico** is a well-known stuntman, stunt coordinator and second-unit director, as well as a special effects coordinator. He has has worked on more than 100 films and TV shows plus many more commercials and music videos. Two of his higher-profile films include *Titanic* and *Harsh Times*. For Plantico, deadly raging fires, high-impact car chases and crashes, and bloody physical fights are all in a day's work. He started his career as a mentee of legendary stuntman and actor Johnny Carpenter.

**Q: What do you consider the absolute most dangerous stunts to do?**

A: Those with fire. Even with all of the new, safer protective clothing and burn gels, it still is real fire and holds the highest risk. I started out doing burns without the gels, mainly because they hadn't been developed yet! I've done over 300 burns, ranging from just an arm or a back burn, to being fully engulfed and leaving flaming footprints. I've gotten scorched a few times and lost some hair, but, with the new gels, a lot of that risk is removed.

**Q: Is there a trick to falling down stairs?**

A: Body control and padding! Stair-falls are an art unto themselves. I feel for the stuntwomen who are called to do them. Typically, stuntwomen are wearing dresses and have much less padding.

**Q: Did you have any training?**

A: When I started out, I was mentored by stuntman/actor Johnny Carpenter. He did stunts and acted in a ton of the old 'B Westerns'. He introduced me to Yakima Canutt and some of the older stunt performers. I feel blessed to have spent time with them, learning from the masters of my craft.

**Q: We've heard of using candy to stand in for glass, but what other products add to the realism?**

A: It's not really candy-glass, anymore. That was unstable and would melt under the lights and get sticky. They have developed resin-type materials that look better, hold up, and break more like real glass. We also use breakaway set pieces, like chairs and tables.

**Q: What are some of the secrets to car-chase scenes? And, where do they get all those cars?**

A: Hire the best drivers you can afford, plan it out to the last skid, get tons of coverage, and wreck a lot of cars. We get the cars from companies that specialize in motion-picture vehicles. Sometimes manufacturers give us cars. I have gotten a ton of cars from police impound yards.

**Q: Do you know of any actors who also make fantastic stuntmen?**

A: I feel that actors are way too valuable to do their own stunts. We get a scratch on our face, and we put on a Band-Aid and keep working. The lead actor gets a scratch and everyone has to wait until it heals. That being said, there are some actors out there who are amazing physical performers. Dwayne 'The Rock' Johnson comes to mind, and, in *Bullitt*, Steve McQueen did a ton of his own driving. He was a professional racecar driver and better than many of the stunt drivers of the day.

**Q: Are there any famous actors who came from stuntage?**

A: Richard Farnsworth was a stuntman in the '30s, before he became an Oscar-nominated actor. Kane Hodder is still a working stuntman but will be most remembered as "Jason" from the *Friday the 13th* films.

**Q: How you ever been seriously hurt doing a fight sequence?**

A: I've broken my nose six times doing film stunts, and all six were when actors punched me! To stage a realistic fight is a lot of work and requires talent and planning. I can stage a great bar-type fight, but the masters are the guys like James Lew and Jeff Imada. They're great martial artists and know how to shoot a scene using camera angles to sell the hits.

**Ky "the Rocket Man" Michaelson** comes from a daredevil family, going back to his great uncle who, in 1905, worked his way through college jumping a bicycle more than 50 feet off a homemade ski jump. Michaelson has been building rockets since 1951. He's attached them to cars, motorcycles, go-karts, snowmobiles, boats, a wheelchair, an oversize runner snow sled, a bicycle and even a port-a-potty - and the darn thing flew! He's also built a Buck Rogers-style rocket pack and an earthbound jetpack to propel his son Curt down drag strips at over 50 mph on roller-skates! On May 17, 2004, Michaelson's Civilian Space eXploration Team became the first amateur group to design, build and launch (with the cooperation of federal authorities and coordination of nearby airports and rail lines) a rocket into space, opening the door for the private sector. The rocket achieved an altitude of 72 miles and a speed of 3,420 mph. Today, Michaelson works with other stuntmen and women, building rockets for car and motorcycle stunts. He's worked on more than 200 feature films and TV shows and has been instrumental in setting 72 state, national, and international speed records with rocket-powered vehicles. He also holds a number of patents for his pioneering work in the stunt and rocket fields.

---

**Q: What kind of emotions and thoughts are going through your head when you're riding one of these rocket-powered vehicles?**

A: Well, a rocket-powered vehicle is dangerous, you know. Speed kills, as they say. It's the sudden stop that gets you, not the speed. But there's always the danger of getting hurt or killed, you know; I mean on the rocket power itself, because you're going very, very fast, and you have to stop. If the parachutes don't come out, you crash, you know, so you have excitement, but you also have fear. When you get through it, all of a sudden you're pretty darn happy, because you gambled again with death, and you made it through it. It's a heck of a sensation to accelerate pretty fast, you know.

**Q: And, how fast do you typically go?**

A: Well, Kitty O'Neil set a world record in my car – she went 412 miles an hour in 3.22 seconds, which is still the world's fastest quarter-mile run.

**Q: How did you incorporate your expertise with rockets into your work in film and television?**

A: Well, I got involved with a stuntman by the name of Dar Robinson through a good friend of mine out on the West Coast who makes parachutes, Jim. He talked to Dar and said, "Yeah, you should get to know Ky Michaelson." And, he said to me, "Yeah, you should to get to know Dar Robinson." So, I started building specialized equipment for Dar to do stunts. At the time, we started working for *That's Incredible*, and then we did a show on Dar, *World's Most Spectacular Stunts*, a one-hour ABC special. We did some stunts and stuff that'd never ever been done before. We brought a lot of the equipment to the industry they'd never seen before that they use to this day. And, when guys are jumping 30-40 feet into an airbag, Dar jumped over 300 feet, and then we started bringing a lot of fire gags into the business.

**Q: You worked with Kitty O'Neil, a famous stuntwoman at a time when most stunts were done by men...**

A: Yeah, I worked with Kitty O'Neil for a number of years. We set the world speed record with cars, and we did a number of stunts together, yes. She was a very athletic person, and she was also totally deaf. One thing that scared me about Kitty is she had no fear, and no fear is not good. I never saw any fear in her. Kitty could read lips, which helped, but she learned how to talk by putting her hands on her mother's vocal chords and the vibrations from it. It's a weird story, but true.

**Q: Is it a totally different aspect... designing stunts for other people and designing rockets for other people to use in their stunts?**

A: Yeah, that's a totally different thing. But, I have a total mechanical photographic mind. I close my eyes and see the stunt and see the equipment that needs to be built. That's my gift.

# JATON

INTERVIEW

**Reno and Cleo Jaton**, daredevils extraordinaire, are a team both on the pavement and off. They are happily married, thanks to an introduction by none other than Jeffery R. Werner, but they also tour the world doing stunt shows together. Reno Jaton is one of Europe's foremost motorcycle stuntmen and Cleo Jaton, after being trained by her husband, is the world's fastest female pavement skier.

**To Reno: How did you break into the movie business?**

A: I was hired on a German movie to change a windshield of a stunt car, which was to hit a pedestrian. The stuntman, who came from France, after seventeen takes, still did not perform as required. The art director called lunch, and I got to speak with the stuntman and the stunt coordinator. They told me, "If you are so good, show us." The stunt coordinator jumped in the car, and I performed the stunt as per the scenario. At this moment, the art director, who had overheard our discussion and stayed out of sight to watch the outcome, walked up to me, slapped me on the back, and said, "You will do the stunts." I turned him down, saying, "You refused to hire me to do stunts on this movie. I am just here to change the windshield. Next time, call me." He did.

**To Cleo: Before meeting Reno, did you ever have any aspirations to do dangerous stunts in front of audiences?**

A: Not professionally. I have always been physically adventurous – gymnastics, dance, rock climbing, etc. – and I found it difficult to pass up a challenge. When Jeff and I met, I was performing in a Western-style stunt show in a theme park, in Branson, Missouri. I was playing the love interest, but, between shows, I talked the stuntmen into teaching me the high fall and other interesting tricks, like how to handle a bullwhip. It was fun.

**To both: Most married couples don't find themselves doing acrobatics on a moving motorcycle at 140 mph or assisting your husband as he is about to be dragged by a jet car going 236 mph with a 700 degree flame flying over his head down a track. What's it like being professional daredevils and be married with a child? Do you fear for each other's safety when you're out there together doing dangerous stunts?**

Cleo: Of course, we fear for each other's safety. We have a very deep love, for which we owe a great deal of thanks to Jeff – he introduced us! However, I knew that Reno was a professional stuntman when I met him, and I respect and trust his enormous skill and experience. I can't remove the fear factor without completely changing who Reno is, and I wouldn't want to do that.

Reno: I fear for Cleo, too, but we never took any chances beyond what I considered our, admittedly narrow, safety margin. It is indescribable: In the middle of a show in front of a screaming crowd, this split second when I see Cleo smiling at me, and we share a very personal, private moment in the middle of chaos.

**To Reno: Could you describe how you trained Cleo to drive motorcycles standing up, and all the other stunts you do together?**

A: Cleo had a wonderful sense of balance and excellent coordination. During our intensive training, she progressed beyond my expectations. She was easy to train. I have rarely met anyone who follows so well directions like "tighten your calves, block your abdominal muscles, etc." while working at high speed. She reproduced exactly the changes of movement, and she progressed by trusting in my direction, even when she didn't immediately understand the purpose. And, as a bonus, we went home each night together!

**To Both: What's more important in the stunt world – training, agility, or pure guts?**

A: I think one without the others would be useless for a professional in the stunt world. Real 'guts' comes from self-confidence. In other words, knowing what you are capable of because of your physical and mental training and experience. It's pretty simple: If you don't have the guts, do something else. But, everyone needs agility, physical and mental training, and, especially, truckloads of motivation. I cannot stress too much the importance of good fitness and constant rehearsal.

**Sandy Gimpel** has been a stunt coordinator and stuntwoman for forty years, with experience on many Hollywood films and television shows. She was responsible for breaking many barriers for women in stunt work, including being the first stuntwoman to earn directing credentials from the Director's Guild of America. She holds a black belt in Karate and stars in her own workout video called *StuntBlasters: Low-impact Cardio Workout,* which combines yoga, martial arts and pilates.

**Q: You've been in the business for 40 years; how did you get started?**

A: I went on an interview for a show called *Lost In Space*, in 1967, and I thought they were looking for someone to stand in, but they were looking for someone to do stunts for someone who was 11 years old (actor Billy Mummy). I had no idea what a stunt was. It wasn't popular like it is today, so he explained to me what it was and said, "There's a gym in Santa Monica, and you go three days a week. You can stand in and do all the stunts for Billy, and you'll be on the show." I was in my early twenties, and I thought, "Cool! What a great job."

**Q: What are some of the difficulties that you face as a female in the business?**

A: Guys hire other guys. It's always tougher for the girls. You'll go out on a show, and there'll be twenty stunt people working, and they will have one or two girls and fifteen guys. It's a guy's world. There's nothing you can do about it.

**Q: Have you ever gotten seriously hurt doing a stunt?**

A: I did a *Kellogg's' Fruit and Fiber* commercial. The shot is of a guy sitting in a tall tower, and he's eating his cereal, and he's up there, because he thinks nobody can steal his stuff. Here's a lady that's going to get it no matter what. She's up in a hot-air balloon, 150 feet in the air, and she bungee jumps backwards out of the hot-air balloon, grabs his cereal, and bounces out of the shot. I had never bungee jumped. I had to be connected around my waist. There was a post outside the balloon for me to stand on. Next, they put me on a crane, and I dropped down to pick up the cereal, but they wanted to do the bungee scene one more time. My adrenaline was then gone, so I'm coming back up, upside down. The bungee cord hit me against my arm and against my leg. The pain felt like a thousand rubber bands hitting me at the same time, and I'm bouncing in the air. When they put me down, my girlfriend was there taking pictures. I had hematoma on my leg that looked like a baseball bat, but the commercial looks amazing.

**Q: You have said it's easier now for high jumps – why?**

A: With technology, there's less danger. They can put you on a thing called an ascender or accelerator, and it will stop you inches above the ground. You still have to know how to hold your body, but you are attached to a cable. You are doing a free fall, and then it slows you to the ground.

**Q: Any funny stories about actors doing their own stunts?**

A: I worked with Jim Carey three times. He's so funny. He almost hit me with a car on *The Truman Show*. We had a line in the street where I was standing that we had rehearsed. The stunt guy was going to do the driving. Jim went, "No, no, no, I want to drive." I told him, "Ok, but if you cross that line, you're going to be so sorry." So, we did the first shot, and he crossed the line. As he passed the line, he threw the car sideways, went up on the curve, almost hit the post – he was so funny. He was worried, because he'd almost hit me. We did the second take, and he was perfect.

**Q: You sometimes get to act and do stunts. Can you give some examples?**

A: I did a stunt on *CSI*, two years ago, in which I played a little old lady that drives a car through a restaurant. It was a full-blown guest-starring role. There I was in the credits. I had lines, because they would flash back to her talking to her family, her grandson, putting on the GPS, and other things before she crashed. They actually did the scene in a real restaurant. They had a tempered-glass window, so, when I crashed the window, there was nobody in there.

**Q: Any advice for women in the business?**

A: Always know what you are doing. Check things, because it's your life out there.

**Johnny Airtime**, born Roger Glennwells Jr., is a stuntman known for extreme and complex motorcycle stunts. He started motocross racing at only 14, turning pro two years later. He performed his first ramp-to-ramp jump in 1984, leaping 100 feet over an 18 wheeler lengthwise in Abilene, Texas. Since then he has executed 4,350 ramp to ramp jumps that were longer than 100 feet without crashing once — the best safety history on record. His lifetime of riding and racing motorcycles prepares him to take on especially challenging stunts and he has broken multiple world records. He also runs the Airtime Association, an organization that monitors and tracks motorcycle-jumping measurement and statistics.

**Q: You go by the name Johnny Airtime. Could you tell us how you got that name?**

A: I got the name Johnny Airtime, because I was in a West Texas Grand Prix, in 1982, and I was flying over so many people's heads, bouncing in midair, and landing in front of them that people started calling me "Mr. Airtime." When I started jumping ramps, I was still in the Air Force, so I couldn't use my real name, because I would be in trouble. So, I had to come up with a new name, and picked Johnny Airtime.

**Q: You worked on a lot of TV shows, including Stunt Masters and *World's Greatest Stunts*, where you jumped head first over a moving train on a motorcycle. Can you talk a little about your experiences on those shows?**

A: On *The World's Greatest Stunts*, they brought in a beautiful train, and I accelerated a motorcycle between the railroad tracks, up to about 70 miles an hour, hit a 16 foot tall ramp, flew through the air over a train, which was an 180 foot jump, and, a half a second after, I jumped off the ramp, the train hit the ramp and destroyed it. The train was moving 25 miles an hour; I was going 70 or 80.

I've done 4350 ramp-to-ramp jumps over 100 feet, so sometimes I forget a few details here and there. On the *Stunt Masters* jump, I rode next to a 20-foot box van down the highway and hit a launch ramp with the landing ramp removed. The box van drove around the launch ramp, F-turned, and straightened up underneath me. I had to lead him, jump ahead, and when I came down he was under there, and I landed on the roof of the box van at about 50-55 miles an hour. I did two, but my latest one was on *Guinness World Records Primetime*.

I also broke the world record for jumping over helicopters. I jumped four with the blades moving.

**Q: What kind of training did you do for this?**

A: While I was racing pro-motor cross in the '70s, I would analyze all the pros and ask them questions. I started learning about how to design ramps, fabrication, and physics, as well as the difference in the conditions will cause the distance to change.

When I'm jumping, I have to take into account ambient air temperature, barometric pressure, density, altitude, humidity, wind direction, wind speed – all these things make a difference on what the bike's going to do.

**Q: How exact do these calculations have to be?**

A: Well, I've put together books which detail every ramp angle and every speed. I have to keep track of all the little things, because changing one little thing can throw you off entirely.

**Q: You've been called both a motorcycle stuntman and a daredevil. Can you talk about what each distinction means, and how you feel about it?**

A: My stunt friends would say that a stuntman can do stunts one after another, and that stuntmen practice, have the right equipment, and are professionals.

A daredevil is an amateur who doesn't know what he is doing. He's just winging it without adequate preparation. But on a movie set, there's a lot of winging it too, because you need the skills coming in, in order to execute the stunts they want. But the stunts they want are usually pretty low-level, unless they are going to give you a lot of time to prepare.

Evel Knievel represented certain things, and I'm diametrically opposed to that in a lot of ways. Everybody's got a different reason for doing what they do, but I did want to be a stuntman in Hollywood.

**Q: So, do you consider yourself more of a stuntman or daredevil?**

A: I don't consider myself a daredevil, at all. I carefully calculate and do stunts. I don't like the word daredevil, and I don't want to act like I'm imitating anybody. I do everything my own way. It's a little different, and I've set some standards. I have the Airtime Association, which lists all the world record holders in motorcycle jumping, any existing record holder in any category.

**Q: The Airtime Association seems really important to you...**

A: It is. I travel to world record attempts and set up the official measurements and give them certificates. I'm trying to give the underdogs – the guys with the real world records – the credit they deserve. Evel Knievel was a master of PR, but there are girls and guys that have jumped much farther than he ever did.

Recently, two girls beat his longest jump by about 30 feet. Everybody that sets the world record in whatever category should have a real title. Guinness only gives one person a world record in motorcycle distance jumping, and they don't consider all the different classes. There's more information on the Airtime Association website, for those interested.

REX